The Joy of Raspberries

by Theresa Millang

Adventure Publications, Inc.
Cambridge, Minnesota

A thank you to all

A special thank you to friends, family and all other contributors to this collection. I have included all my favorite recipes, using fresh, frozen, canned and dried raspberries.

Book and Cover Design by Jonathan Norberg

10 9 8 7 6 5 4 3 2 1

Copyright 2009 by Theresa Nell Millang
Published by Adventure Publications, Inc.
820 Cleveland Street South
Cambridge, Minnesota 55008
1-800-678-7006
www.adventurepublications.net
Printed in China
ISBN-13: 978-1-59193-235-2
ISBN-10: 1-59193-235-1

Table of Contents

BREADS, MUFFINS AND SCONES

SALADS

SIDES

CAKES, CUPCAKES, SHORTCAKES, COFFEECAKES AND CHEESECAKES

Cakes

Cupcakes

Shortcakes

Bars

DESSERTS

FROZEN DESSERTS

PASTRIES, TORTES AND TARTS

Pastries

Tortes

Tarts

PIES

PRESERVES, JAM, JELLY AND MARMALADE

Preserves

Jam

Jelly

Introduction

I always look forward to raspberries, the plump and juicy perennial summer favorite. Sweet with a slight tangy tart flavor and a melt-in-your-mouth texture, raspberries are a delicious favorite that always remind me of summer. The best way to have an abundance of raspberries is to grow them in a backyard patch. Short of that, many growers will let you pick your own raspberries. If you can, visit such a berry farm, as it's a wonderful experience. Don't worry about wasting berries either, as you can use the fresh berries right away and easily freeze some for another time. If you don't have time to actually visit a berry farm, fruit stands on the street and open-air markets are filled with beautiful raspberries during the summer months, and raspberries are available in most supermarkets year-round. Dried raspberries are sometimes available in natural food stores, food co-ops, some of the large buying clubs and online.

Raspberries aren't only delicious, they're also very versatile and highly nutritious. In *The Joy of Raspberries*, I include delicious recipes for appetizers, salads, breads, ice cream, cakes, desserts, meals, cheesecake, pastries, muffins, tortes, bars, soup, sides and so much more. I have included recipes that use fresh, frozen, dried or canned raspberries. I have included all of my favorite recipes and recipes I have collected from across our great country. Enjoy!

History of Raspberries

A member of the rose family, people have been enjoying raspberries since prehistoric times. Thought to have originated in eastern Asia, wild raspberries have been widely cultivated across Europe for many years. In fact, the historical record is replete with references to raspberries, and various cultures (especially the Romans) helped encourage cultivation in Europe. Widespread cultivation in the Americas didn't happen until later, but by the nineteenth century, significant amounts of raspberries were being grown in North America.

In the United States, the Pacific Northwest states of Washington, Oregon and California account for almost all raspberry production. In fact, Washington State accounts for nearly 50% of the U.S. production of red raspberries. Other commercial producers of raspberries include Russia, Poland, Germany, Chile and eastern Europe.

Health Benefits of Raspberries

Raspberries not only taste good, but they're healthy too. Nearly fat-free, raspberries contain no cholesterol or sodium, and they are rich in vitamins and minerals, including vitamin C, folate, iron and potassium. Raspberries also provide high amounts of insoluble fiber and a significant amount of pectin, which helps control cholesterol levels.

Raspberries also contain a variety of antioxidants. Quercetin and ellagic acid are just two examples, but there are many others. The health benefits of these antioxidants are not completely known, but preliminary research indicates that raspberries are even healthier than we thought. Raspberries are currently being studied for their cancer-fighting ability, as well as for their potential to help prevent inflammation, heart and circulatory diseases, and age-related decline. Thankfully, cooking doesn't destroy these helpful chemicals, so you can enjoy your raspberries hot or cold.

Selection and Storage

Because raspberries are highly perishable, try to purchase them just prior to use, preferably one or two days early. Choose raspberries that are firm, plump and deep in color. If you're buying pre-packaged berries, be sure to inspect your berries and watch out for containers with moldy berries. If you're buying in bulk, store berries loosely in covered containers. Do not wash berries until ready to be used, and don't leave them at room temperature or exposed to sunlight for too long, as this will tend to cause them to spoil. Instead, refrigerate berries at 32–40°.

Preparing Raspberries for Freezing

If you're not planning to use your raspberries immediately or want to save them for future use, freeze them. Raspberries freeze well and frozen raspberries keep for six months to a year. To prepare them for freezing, make sure to select berries that are fully ripe with a rich, red color and remove any mushy, discolored, moldy or immature fruit. Clean the berries by putting them in a colander and immersing them in cold water two or three times. Drain well.

Four Ways to Freeze Raspberries

There are several different ways to freeze raspberries. Each freezing method produces different results and each is best suited for particular uses; in order to provide you with as many options as possible, I've included four of the most popular methods here.

Unsweetened Dry Freezing
This method will produce separately frozen berries. After rinsing the raspberries, dry them completely by placing them on paper towels and gently pat them dry. Let them air-dry for a few minutes. Then place them in a single layer on parchment paper or wax paper on a tray and place it in the freezer. Once frozen, place the berries in a plastic freezer bag, leaving about 1 inch of headspace. Try to get as much air out of the bag as possible before sealing it; then seal it and return it to the freezer immediately.

Unsweetened Dry Pack Freezing
Using this method produces bunches of berries that are frozen together. Place rinsed and dried berries into freezer containers or bags, removing as much air as possible when sealing. Leave enough headspace in the containers for expansion, a ½ inch is usually enough. Place containers in freezer.

Sugar Pack Freezing
Although not necessary, some people prefer to freeze their berries with sugar. Sugar Pack Freezing is best used in pies, as the fruit freezes in a solid block. Some berry enthusiasts feel that freezing with sugar helps the berries retain better color and texture, as the sugar combines with the raspberries' natural juices, creating a syrup that protects the berries from exposure to air. To freeze raspberries with sugar, add ½ –¾ cup of sugar to every 7–8 quarts of dry berries. When combining the berries and sugar, stir carefully to avoid damaging the berries, and mix until most of the sugar is dissolved. Place berries in containers, leaving enough headspace for expansion, and then freeze. Note: It's best to use plastic containers when using this method, but freezer bags can be used, if necessary. Be warned, however, that using freezer bags can be messy.

Syrup Pack Freezing

Similar to Sugar Pack Freezing, this method involves a syrup mixture and results in a solid block of frozen fruit. To create the syrup, combine 1 cup of sugar and 1 cup of water and mix well. Heat the mixture to dissolve the sugar, then chill the finished syrup. After placing the berries in freezer containers, cover the berries with the chilled syrup. Be sure to leave enough headspace in the containers for expansion, then seal and place them in freezer.

Using Frozen Raspberries

You can substitute frozen berries for fresh berries in many recipes, but when you're using frozen berries, don't forget to account for any sugar that was used during freezing, as this sugar will alter the taste of the final recipe. In addition, when preparing to use frozen berries, note that thawing berries slowly will often produce soft, mushy fruit that tastes fine, but doesn't retain its shape. Such berries will work well in baked goods and other recipes, but if you want your berries to retain their shape, try using the microwave to thaw them halfway (taking care not to cook them). The time required to do this varies with the microwave and the amount of berries, so start by microwaving a small amount of berries on a low setting for a short amount of time. Then add time as you see fit; it may take some trial and error to get the settings just right.

Using Dried Raspberries

Because raspberries are highly perishable, using dried raspberries is a great way to prepare delicious raspberry dishes any time of year. While not readily available in all grocery stores, dried raspberries can usually be found in natural food stores, food co-ops, some of the large buying clubs and online.

You can use dried raspberries without preparation, or you can reconstitute them. To reconstitute, cover the berries with water in a pot and let them soak for several hours. After soaking, they should be ready to use. When reconstituting raspberries, one cup of dried berries will produce about 1½ cups of berries.

Raspberry Equivalents

1 pint fresh (2 cups) weighs approximately ¾ pound
1 pint fresh yields four servings
2 pints fresh (4 cups) needed for one 9-inch pie
1¼ cups fresh = one 10-ounce package frozen raspberries
Approximately 3 to 4 cups fresh raspberries = 1 cup dried raspberries

Planting and Growing Raspberries

Raspberry plants are biennial, which means they produce canes (woody stems) during the first growing season; lateral branches grow from these canes, which produce fruit the following year and then die. For this reason, when discussing raspberry propagation, it's often common to hear references to "first-year" and "second-year" wood. Remember, first-year plants produce canes. Lateral branches will grow from these canes, which will produce fruit a year later.

Of the many varieties of raspberries cultivated today, all are either summer-bearing or fall-bearing. Established summer-bearing plants produce one large crop a year during the summer. Fall-bearing plants (commonly referred to as ever-bearing) produce two crops, one in the midsummer and another in fall. Ever-bearing plants differ from summer-bearing crops in that their first-year canes produce fruit. For this reason, they are quite popular. Ever-bearing plants are hardy throughout much of the nation if they are cut to the ground each autumn and then mulched.

When planting raspberries, place each plant 20 inches away from one another in rows 5 feet apart. Be sure to plant them in areas with a good deal of organic material and good drainage. Raspberries cannot stand wet ground, so if your soil is wet or poorly-drained, plant your raspberries on a mound 18 inches above the water table. When planting, plant them with well-rotted manure, and fertilize with additional manure the season after that.

What to Expect

If you're planting them from seed, don't expect them to produce right away; it usually takes 1–2 years before they bear fruit. For every foot of planted raspberries in each row, expect 2 pounds of fruit. Replace your raspberry plants every 10–15 years, as they are less productive when older.

Pruning and Upkeep Tips

In order to ensure that red raspberry plants keep producing fruit, you need to prune your plants appropriately. Generally speaking, it's best to prune raspberries twice a year. The first pruning should occur before the plants develop leaves in early spring. During this pruning, you should remove all weak and damaged canes, leaving 6–14 healthy branches. When doing so, it's best to dispose of canes that are high off the ground, as canes closer to the root system will obtain more nourishment, which will maximize fruit production. The second pruning should occur immediately after the harvest. Cut all of the old canes (second-year wood) down to the ground level; be sure to cut these down completely; leaving "stubs" or remnants of the canes will foster disease and encourage insect growth. Do not prune the first-year canes until the following season, as they will be your fruit producers the next year.

Of course, growing strategies vary by region and by species, so be sure to contact your local county extension service for more complete growing details.

Sources: Cornell Fruit Resources. "Cornell Fruit Resources." Cornell University. www.fruit.cornell.edu/Berries/bramble.html (Accessed 05/06/09); HE-0360. "Drying Fruits at Home." Alabama Cooperative Extension Service, Alabama A & M and Auburn Universities. www.aces.edu/pubs/docs/H/HE-0360/ (Accessed 05/06/09); Introduction to Fruit Crops. "Introduction to Fruit Crops." Ed. Mark Rieger. University of Georgia. www.uga.edu/fruit/rubus.html (Accessed 05/06/09); Nutritiondata.com "Nutrition Facts and Analysis for Raspberries." www.nutritiondata.com/facts/fruits-and-fruit-juices/2053/2 (Accessed 05/06/09); The North American Bramble Growers Association. "Freezing Raspberries and Blackberries." www.raspberrryblackberry.com (Accessed 5/14/09)

Appetizers

BAKED BRIE BITES

Puff pastry filled with warm cheese, raspberry jam and toasted pecans. A great holiday appetizer . . .

1 package (9.5 ounces) mini puff pastry shells
2 tablespoons seedless raspberry jam
1 8-ounce Brie cheese, cut into 24 pieces
1 tablespoon toasted pecans, chopped

Bake, cool and remove tops of shells following package directions.
Reduce heat to 350°.

Place ⅛ teaspoon jam and 1 piece of cheese in each shell. Sprinkle with pecans. Place shells on a baking sheet. Bake about 5 minutes or until cheese melts. Serve immediately. Refrigerate leftovers.

Makes 24 servings.

BERRY DIP

Silken tofu is used in this berry good dip!

1 10-ounce package frozen raspberries in syrup, thawed, syrup reserved
1 10.5-ounce package silken tofu
1 tablespoon honey

Rub thawed raspberries through a strainer to remove seeds; discard seeds.

Process strained raspberries, reserved syrup, tofu and honey in a blender until smooth. Place mix into a serving bowl. Serve with fresh fruit. Store in the refrigerator.

Makes 8 servings.

CAJUN CHICKEN BITES WITH RASPBERRY DIPPING SAUCE

Cajun chicken bites with dipping sauce . . . just the appetizer for that football game!

1½ cups all-purpose flour
1 cup finely chopped pecans
1 tablespoon dried oregano
2 teaspoons ground cumin
1 teaspoon dried thyme
½ teaspoon cayenne pepper
1 teaspoon salt

12 tablespoons corn oil, divided

4 whole, skinless, boneless chicken
   breasts, cut into 1-inch pieces

Dipping Sauce
1 cup seedless red raspberry jam
2 tablespoons Dijon-style mustard
   or to taste
a few drops Tabasco hot pepper
   sauce, or to taste

Mix first seven ingredients in a shallow dish.

Place 6 tablespoons corn oil in a small bowl. Dip each chicken piece first in oil, then in flour mixture until well coated.

Heat 3 tablespoons oil at a time in a large skillet over medium heat. Add half of the coated chicken pieces; stir and cook until browned and cooked through. Remove from skillet; keep warm in oven. Repeat with remaining oil and chicken. Refrigerate leftover chicken and dipping sauce.

Dipping Sauce: Mix all ingredients in a serving bowl until blended.

Spear chicken bites with toothpicks, and serve with dipping sauce.

Makes 8 servings.

FRUITY BRIE

An attractive, delicious appetizer.

3 teaspoons butter, softened
1 8-ounce package baby Brie
6 teaspoons raspberry preserves
3 teaspoons sliced almonds

Preheat oven to 350°.

Spread butter on top of Brie. Spread preserves on top of butter. Top evenly with almonds. Bake 10–15 minutes. Serve warm with French bread or crackers. Refrigerate leftovers.

Makes 8 servings.

RASPBERRY GLAZED WINGS

Love those tasty wings.

1½ cups seedless raspberry jam
½ cup cider vinegar
½ cup light soy sauce
6 garlic cloves, minced
2 teaspoons freshly ground black pepper
3 pounds chicken wings cut into three sections; discard tips

Mix jam, vinegar, soy sauce, garlic and black pepper in a large saucepan. Bring to a boil over medium heat. Boil 1 minute.

Place wings in a large bowl. Add half the raspberry mixture to bowl; toss until coated. Reserve remaining mixture.

Line a 15x10x1-inch baking pan with aluminum cooking foil; grease foil well. Remove wings from marinade and place in pan. Discard marinade. Bake wings uncovered at 375° for 30 minutes, turning once.

While wings are baking, bring reserved raspberry mixture to a boil in a small saucepan. Reduce heat and simmer uncovered 10–15 minutes or until thickened. Brush wings with mixture. Bake, turning and basting once, 20–25 minutes or until juices run clear. Serve warm. Refrigerate leftovers.

Makes 10 servings.

RED ANTS ON A LOG

Celery stuffed with goat cheese, pomegranate and raspberry . . . a tangy, sweet and savory appetizer.

4 ounces goat cheese, softened to room temperature
4 teaspoons chopped green onion tops
4 teaspoons chopped capers (optional)
6 large celery stalks, trimmed of strings and cut into 4 pieces each
¼ cup arils (seed sacs) from one pomegranate
¼ cup dried raspberries

Mix goat cheese, green onion tops, and capers in a bowl. Fill each piece of celery with mixture. Press pomegranate arils and dried raspberries onto the cheese mixture. Serve cold. Refrigerate leftovers.

Makes 24 servings.

See page 63 for tips on removing the arils from a pomegranate.

Beverages

MANGO RASPBERRY SMOOTHIE

Share this tasty treat with a friend.

1 ripe mango, peeled, pitted and cubed
1 cup fresh or frozen raspberries
1 cup raspberry frozen yogurt
1 cup ice cubes
¼ cup fruit juice (orange or raspberry cranberry)

Place all ingredients in a blender container; blend until smooth. Serve immediately in chilled glasses.

Makes 2 servings.

MINT FLAVORED RASPBERRY TEA

Mint and raspberries flavor this refreshing iced tea.

4 cups boiling water
5 tea bags, green
¼ cup mint leaves, crushed
¼ cup granulated sugar
1 32-ounce bottle cran-raspberry beverage
fresh raspberries

Steep tea bags and mint in 4 cups boiling water in a 2-quart pot for 10 minutes.
Remove bags and mint. Stir in sugar until dissolved. Stir in cran-raspberry beverage.
Pour mixture into a heatproof pitcher. Serve over ice. Garnish with fresh raspberries
as desired.

Makes 8 servings.

PINK BERRY LEMONADE

Pink lemonade . . . a refreshing treat.

¾ cup granulated sugar
1 cup fresh lemon juice
6 cups cold water
1 cup fresh or frozen raspberries, pureed, strained
 and seeds discarded

ice cubes
thin lemon slices

Mix sugar, lemon juice and water in a large pitcher until sugar is completely dissolved. Stir in raspberry puree. Chill well.

Serve over ice cubes; garnish with lemon slices. Refrigerate leftovers.

Makes 6 servings.

Breads
Muffins
Scones

ALMOND RASPBERRY QUICK BREAD

Enjoy a slice of this delicate bread plain or with softened butter.

2 cups all-purpose flour
2 teaspoons baking powder
½ teaspoon baking soda
¾ teaspoon salt

½ cup butter or margarine, softened
1 cup granulated sugar
2 large eggs
½ teaspoon pure vanilla extract
½ teaspoon pure almond extract
¾ cup dairy sour cream
½ cup slivered almonds, toasted
1 cup fresh raspberries, rinsed and patted dry

Preheat oven to 350°.
Generously grease a 9x5-inch loaf pan.

Mix flour, baking powder, baking soda and salt in a large bowl; set aside.

Beat butter and sugar in a mixing bowl on high speed until light and fluffy. Beat in eggs, one at a time. Beat in extracts. Reduce speed to low, then sprinkle in dry ingredients, alternating with the sour cream. Beat until well moistened. Stir in almonds and raspberries by hand.

Pour batter into prepared pan. Bake 50–60 minutes or until a wooden pick inserted in the center comes out clean. Cover with aluminum baking foil the last 10 minutes of baking time if browning too fast.

Cool in pan 10 minutes, then remove from pan and cool completely on a wire rack before slicing. Refrigerate leftovers.

Makes 1 loaf.

CHERRY RASPBERRY MINI LOAVES

Dried raspberries and dried cherries are used in these small loaves. Spread cooled sliced bread with softened butter mixed in a bowl with raspberry or cherry preserves.

3 cups all-purpose flour
2 teaspoons baking powder
1 teaspoon baking soda
1 teaspoon salt
¼ teaspoon ground cloves

1 cup granulated sugar
¾ cup butter, softened
2 tablespoons brown sugar, packed
1 tablespoon honey
1½ teaspoons pure vanilla extract
2 large eggs

1 cup buttermilk
1 cup slivered almonds, toasted
½ cup dried cherries
½ cup dried raspberries

Preheat oven to 350°.
Generously grease five 5½x3-inch mini loaf pans.

Mix first five ingredients in a medium bowl; set aside.

Beat granulated sugar, butter, brown sugar, honey and vanilla extract in a large mixing bowl on medium speed until creamy. Beat in eggs, one at a time. Reduce speed to low.

Gradually beat in flour mixture alternately with buttermilk until well mixed. Stir in almonds and dried fruit by hand.

Spoon batter evenly into prepared pans. Bake 30–40 minutes or until a wooden pick inserted in center comes out clean. Cool in pan 10 minutes, then remove from pan; cool completely. Refrigerate leftovers.

Makes 5 loaves.

DRIED RASPBERRY ALMOND BREAD

The bread machine makes it easy to enjoy this fruity nut bread.

¾ cup whole milk
1 tablespoon butter or margarine
1 large egg
¾ teaspoon salt
2 cups bread flour
⅓ cup dried raspberries
¼ cup toasted slivered almonds
1 tablespoon granulated sugar
1½ teaspoons bread machine yeast

Add ingredients to bread machine pan in order suggested by the manufacturer, adding dried raspberries and almonds with flour.

Use basic/white bread cycle.

Makes one 1-pound loaf.

JULEKAGE

A delicious Scandinavian holiday mixed fruit bread.

1 package active dry yeast
¼ cup warm water (105° to 115°)
¾ cup whole milk, heated in a saucepan
    to 105°
¼ cup butter, cut into pieces
3¼ cups all-purpose flour
    (approximate), divided
⅔ cup chopped mixed candied fruit
½ cup golden raisins
⅓ cup dried raspberries
⅓ cup slivered almonds
¼ cup granulated sugar

1 egg
1 teaspoon pure vanilla extract
½ teaspoon salt
½ teaspoon ground cardamom
½ teaspoon freshly grated
    lemon peel

Glaze
1 cup powdered sugar
2 tablespoons whole milk
    (approximate)

Mix yeast in warm water until dissolved in a small bowl; let stand 5 minutes. Stir butter into warm milk until melted. Place yeast mixture and milk mixture into a large bowl. Stir in 2 cups flour, candied fruit, raisins, raspberries, almonds, sugar, egg, vanilla, salt, cardamom and lemon peel. Beat on medium speed until smooth. Stir in enough remaining flour by hand to make dough easy to handle. Knead dough on a lightly floured surface until smooth and elastic (about 5 minutes). Place in a greased bowl, turning greased side up. Cover and let rise until double in size, about 1½ hours. (Dough is ready if indentation remains when touched.)

Punch down dough. Shape into a round loaf. Place in a greased 9-inch round cake pan. Brush top with melted butter. Cover and let rise until double in size, about 1 hour.

Preheat oven to 350°.
Bake 35–45 minutes or until golden brown. Remove from pan immediately.
Cool completely on a wire rack.

Glaze: Mix powdered sugar and enough milk in a small bowl to a glazing consistency. Spread over bread. Refrigerate leftovers.

Makes 1 loaf.

RASPBERRY APRICOT BREAD

A tasty treat for breakfast or a midnight snack!

2¼ cups bread flour, divided
2 tablespoons granulated sugar
1 package rapid rise yeast
2 teaspoons freshly grated lemon peel
1 teaspoon salt

½ cup whole milk
¼ cup water
2 tablespoons butter or margarine
1 large egg
⅓ cup dried raspberries
⅓ cup coarsely chopped dried apricot

Mix ¾ cup flour, sugar, undissolved yeast, lemon peel and salt in a large mixing bowl; set aside.

Heat milk, water and butter in a small saucepan until very warm (120°–130°). Gradually add mixture to flour mixture. Beat 2 minutes on medium speed.

Add egg and ½ cup flour; beat 2 minutes on high speed. Stir in remaining flour, raspberries and apricots by hand to make a stiff batter.

Spread batter evenly in a greased 8½x4½-inch loaf pan. Cover with a clean kitchen towel; let rise in a draft-free, warm place until doubled in size (about 1 hour).

Preheat oven to 375°.
Bake 30–35 minutes. Remove from pan; cool on a wire rack.

Makes 1 loaf.

CHOCOLATE CHUNK
RASPBERRY MUFFINS

Chocolate and raspberries in these tasty muffins.

2 cups all-purpose flour
¾ cup granulated sugar
1 tablespoon baking powder
¼ teaspoon salt

2 eggs, slightly beaten
½ cup whole milk
½ teaspoon pure vanilla extract
⅓ cup corn oil
1 6-ounce container raspberry yogurt

1 10-ounce package frozen red raspberries in syrup, thawed,
   drained, discard syrup
1¾ cups semi-sweet chocolate chunks (11.5-ounce package)
½ cup chopped pecans

Preheat oven to 400°.
Lightly spray twenty 2½-inch muffin cups with nonstick cooking spray.

Mix flour, sugar, baking powder and salt in a medium bowl.

Mix eggs, milk, vanilla extract, corn oil and yogurt in another medium bowl. Add mixture to flour mixture. Stir just until moistened. Fold in raspberries and chocolate chunks. Spoon batter into prepared muffin cups. Sprinkle tops evenly with pecans.

Bake 18–20 minutes or until a wooden pick inserted in center comes out clean. Cool in pan on a wire rack 5 minutes. Remove muffins; cool completely on a wire rack. Serve warm. Refrigerate leftovers.

Makes 20 muffins.

LEMON RASPBERRY MUFFINS

Makes a good breakfast treat . . . midnight snack too!

1 15-ounce package lemon poppy seed muffin mix
1 cup cold water
¼ cup corn oil
1 egg
1 cup fresh raspberries

1 tablespoon granulated sugar
1 teaspoon ground cinnamon
½ teaspoon ground nutmeg

Preheat oven to 425°.
Paper line a 12-cup muffin pan.

Mix muffin mix, water, corn oil and egg in a large bowl just until blended. Gently stir in raspberries. Spoon batter equally into prepared muffin cups.

Mix sugar, cinnamon and nutmeg in a small bowl; sprinkle mixture over tops of muffins. Bake 14–16 minutes or until light golden brown. Cool in pan 5 minutes. Remove from pan; cool on a wire rack.

Makes 12 muffins.

OAT BRAN RASPBERRY MUFFINS

Bits of raspberries, almonds and coconut in this cholesterol-free muffin. Serve plain or with a little honey, if desired.

Dry Ingredients
½ cup oat bran
2 cups all-purpose flour
½ cup granulated sugar
2½ teaspoons baking powder
½ teaspoon salt
1 tablespoon non-fat dry milk
½ cup toasted whole almonds,
    coarsely chopped

Wet Ingredients
2 egg whites beaten with 1 teaspoon
    corn oil in a small bowl
1 cup skim milk
¼ cup margarine, melted
1 teaspoon fresh lemon juice
1 teaspoon pure vanilla extract
½ cup flaked coconut
1 cup fresh or frozen raspberries

Preheat oven to 400°.
Paper line a 12-cup muffin pan.

Mix all dry ingredients in a large bowl.

Mix all wet ingredients in a medium bowl.

Combine dry and wet ingredients. Stir only to moisten, but batter will be lumpy. Spoon into prepared muffin cups.

Bake 20–25 minutes. Remove from pan. Cool on a wire rack. Serve warm or at room temperature. Refrigerate leftovers.

Makes 12 muffins.

Recipe adapted from my book *The Muffins Are Coming*.

POPPY SEED RASPBERRY MUFFINS

A lovely muffin for a brunch table.

2¼ cups cake flour
1 teaspoon baking soda
½ teaspoon baking powder

⅔ cup granulated sugar
½ cup butter, room temperature
1 tablespoon pure vanilla extract
5 large egg yolks
1 cup dairy sour cream
¼ cup poppy seeds

3 large egg whites, beaten in a bowl with ¼ teaspoon cream
   of tartar and ½ cup granulated sugar until stiff peaks form
3 cups fresh raspberries

Preheat oven to 350°.
Butter and flour twenty-four ⅓-cup muffin cups.

Mix flour, baking soda and baking powder into a medium bowl; set aside.

Beat ⅔ cup sugar and butter in a large bowl until blended. Beat in vanilla extract. Beat in egg yolks, one at a time. Beat mixture until light and pale yellow. Beat in sour cream and poppy seeds. Add flour mixture. Mix well.

Gently fold in egg white mixture. Stir in raspberries. Spoon batter into prepared muffin cups, dividing equally.

Bake about 20–25 minutes or until a wooden pick inserted in center comes out clean. Remove muffins from cups; cool on a wire rack. Serve warm or at room temperature. Refrigerate leftovers.

Makes 24 muffins.

RASPBERRY CREAM CHEESE MUFFINS

Variation: Use frozen raspberries.

2 3-ounce packages cream cheese, softened
⅓ cup butter, softened
1½ cups granulated sugar
1½ teaspoons pure vanilla extract
2 large egg whites
1 large egg

2 cups all-purpose flour
1 teaspoon baking powder
¼ teaspoon baking soda
½ teaspoon salt

½ cup buttermilk
2 cups fresh raspberries
¼ cup finely chopped walnuts or pecans

Preheat oven to 350°.
Foil line 24 muffin cups.

Beat cream cheese and butter in a large bowl on high speed until blended. Beat in sugar. Beat in vanilla, egg whites and egg until well blended.

Mix flour, baking powder, baking soda and salt in a bowl. On low speed, gradually add dry mixture to creamed mixture, alternately with buttermilk. Fold in raspberries and walnuts. Spoon batter evenly into prepared cups.

Bake about 25 minutes or until a wooden pick inserted in center comes out clean. Remove from pan. Cool on a wire rack. Store in refrigerator.

Makes 24 muffins.

WHITE CHOCOLATE RASPBERRY MUFFINS

Fresh or frozen raspberries may be used in this recipe. Do not thaw if frozen raspberries are used.

2 cups all-purpose flour
⅓ cup granulated sugar
1 tablespoon baking powder
¾ teaspoon salt

1 cup whole milk
½ cup butter, melted
1 teaspoon pure vanilla extract
1 egg, slightly beaten

1 cup raspberries
3 ounces coarsely chopped
    white chocolate baking bar

melted butter
granulated sugar

Preheat oven to 400°.

Paper line a 12-cup muffin pan.

Mix flour, ⅓ cup sugar, baking powder and salt in a medium bowl.

Mix milk, butter, vanilla and egg in a large bowl. Stir in flour mixture just until moistened. Stir in raspberries and chopped chocolate. Spoon batter equally into prepared muffin cups.

Bake 20–28 minutes or until golden brown. Remove from oven. Cool 4 minutes in pan, then remove from pan to a wire rack.

Brush top of muffins with melted butter and sprinkle with granulated sugar as desired. Refrigerate leftovers.

Makes 12 muffins.

CHOCOLATE CHIP RASPBERRY SCONES

These scones will become a favorite for that special coffee break.

1¾ cups all-purpose flour
3 tablespoons granulated sugar
2½ teaspoons baking powder
½ teaspoon salt
⅓ cup cold butter, cut into small pieces

½ cup semi-sweet chocolate chips
⅓ cup dried raspberries
2 eggs, divided
½ teaspoon pure vanilla extract
5 tablespoons half-and-half (approximate)

Preheat oven to 400°.

Mix flour, sugar, baking powder and salt in a medium bowl. Cut in butter with a pastry blender until coarse crumbs form.

Stir in chocolate chips, raspberries, 1 egg, vanilla extract and enough half-and-half to form a dough that leaves sides of bowl.

Gently knead dough 10 times on a floured surface. Roll dough into a 9-inch circle. Cut dough into 12 wedges. Place onto an ungreased baking sheet. Beat remaining egg in a small bowl; brush over wedges.

Bake until golden brown, about 9–12 minutes. Remove from oven and immediately remove scones from baking sheet to a cooling rack.

Makes 1 dozen.

RASPBERRY CRANBERRY SCONES

Serve these warm scones for a special breakfast treat, with orange marmalade or raspberry jam. Buttered, of course.

1¾ cups all-purpose flour
5 tablespoons granulated sugar,
   divided
2½ teaspoons baking powder
⅛ teaspoon salt
2 teaspoons freshly grated
   orange peel
⅓ cup butter, cut into small pieces

¼ cup dried raspberries
¼ cup dried cranberries
2 eggs, divided
1 teaspoon pure vanilla extract
⅓ cup half-and-half (approximate)

Preheat oven to 400°.

Mix flour, 3 tablespoons granulated sugar, baking powder, salt and orange peel in a medium bowl. Cut in butter until fine crumbs form.

Stir in raspberries, cranberries, 1 egg, vanilla extract and just enough half-and-half to form dough that leaves sides of the bowl.

Gently knead dough on a lightly floured surface 10 times. Roll dough into a 9-inch circle. Place dough onto an ungreased baking sheet. Cut dough into 12 wedges, but do not separate the wedges.

Beat remaining egg in a small bowl; brush tops of wedges. Sprinkle with remaining 2 tablespoons granulated sugar.

Bake until golden brown, about 16–18 minutes. Remove from oven. Cut wedges apart and remove immediately from baking sheet to a serving plate. Serve warm. Refrigerate leftovers.

Makes 1 dozen.

Salads

CALIFORNIA CHICKEN SALAD

Pistachios and dried raspberries are the surprise ingredients in this delicious salad. Serve with warm rolls.

Dressing
1 clove garlic, minced
1 teaspoon prepared Dijon-style mustard
1 tablespoon balsamic vinegar
juice of 1 large orange, freshly squeezed

Salad
3 cups mixed salad greens, washed and patted dry
1 8-ounce chicken breast, grilled and thinly sliced
1 tart apple, cored, quartered and sliced
½ cup bleu cheese, crumbled
½ cup shelled pistachios
⅓ cup dried raspberries

Dressing: Mix all dressing ingredients in a small bowl; whisk to blend.

Salad: Divide greens equally among four salad plates. Place equal portions of chicken, apple, bleu cheese, pistachios and dried raspberries over greens. Drizzle with salad dressing. Serve. Refrigerate leftovers.

Makes 4 servings.

CHICKEN SALAD IN TOMATO BOATS

Dried raspberries and dried cranberries add a special flavor. Serve with warm rolls or crunchy bread sticks.

Salad
2 cups cubed cooked chicken
½ cup mayonnaise
½ teaspoon paprika
⅓ cup dried raspberries
⅓ cup dried cranberries
½ cup chopped celery
1 green onion, chopped
¼ cup minced green bell pepper
½ cup chopped pecans
½ teaspoon seasoning salt
freshly ground black pepper to taste

4 large ripe tomatoes, seeded, with tops cut down about 2 inches

Mix all ingredients except tomatoes in a medium bowl. Chill 1 hour, then spoon mixture into tomatoes. Serve. Refrigerate leftovers.

Makes 4 servings.

CHICKEN SPINACH SALAD WITH WARM RASPBERRY DRESSING

A delicious salad dressed with warm raspberry balsamic vinaigrette.

Raspberry Balsamic Vinaigrette
2 tablespoons olive oil
½ cup red raspberry jam
1 tablespoon Dijon-style mustard
1½ tablespoons balsamic vinegar

Salad
4 fully cooked, grilled, boneless, skinless chicken breasts
8 cups baby spinach leaves
1 red bell pepper cut into thin strips

1 cup sliced mushrooms
¼ cup thinly sliced red onion
½ cup fresh raspberries, rinsed and patted dry
2 hard boiled egg whites, chopped

Vinaigrette: Heat olive oil in a small saucepan. Stir in jam, mustard and vinegar; heat thoroughly.

Salad: Toss chicken, spinach and red pepper strips with warm dressing; divide among 4 large serving plates. Place mushrooms, onions, raspberries and egg whites on top. Serve. Refrigerate leftovers.

Makes 4 servings.

CURRIED CHICKEN SALAD

Serve with warm, crusty rolls . . . buttered, of course.

6 slices bacon, cooked and crumbled
3 cups diced, cooked chicken
½ cup chopped celery
1 cup seedless grapes
⅓ cup dried raspberries

Dressing
1 cup mayonnaise
2 tablespoons minced red onion
1 teaspoon fresh lemon juice
½ teaspoon Worcestershire sauce
½ teaspoon curry powder
¼ teaspoon freshly ground black pepper
salt to taste

Mix first five ingredients in a large salad bowl.

Dressing: Whisk all dressing ingredients in a bowl; pour dressing over salad and toss. Chill slightly before serving. Refrigerate leftovers.

Makes 8 servings.

FRUITED CHICKEN SALAD WITH RASPBERRY VINAIGRETTE

Serve with warm poppy seed raspberry muffins.

Vinaigrette
⅓ cup extra virgin olive oil
¼ cup raspberry vinegar
1½ tablespoons Dijon-style mustard
1 tablespoon granulated sugar
¼ teaspoon salt
¼ teaspoon freshly ground black pepper

Salad
2 7-ounce bags of butter lettuce blend salad greens
1 11-ounce can mandarin oranges, well drained
3 cups fully cooked grilled chicken breast strips
⅓ cup sliced green onions
⅓ cup crumbled feta cheese
1 cup fresh raspberries, rinsed and patted dry

Vinaigrette: Whisk all vinaigrette ingredients in a small bowl; set aside.

Salad: Place lettuce, oranges, chicken, onions and cheese in a large salad bowl. Add vinaigrette; toss. Add raspberries; toss lightly. Serve immediately. Refrigerate leftovers.

Makes 6 servings.

HAM AND CHEESE FRESH FRUIT SALAD

Perfect for that patio luncheon. Serve with warm rolls and iced tea.
Hint: Use chicken or turkey in place of ham.

Salad
1½ cups cubed cooked ham
2 fresh peaches, peeled and sliced
1 10-ounce package mixed salad greens (6 cups)
1 pint fresh strawberries, rinsed, patted dry, hulled and sliced
½ cup fresh raspberries, rinsed and patted dry
1 cup deli Swiss shredded cheese or American cheese

Dressing
¼ cup fresh orange juice
2 tablespoons corn oil
1 tablespoon white wine vinegar
½ teaspoon poppy seed
¼ teaspoon salt

Salad: Mix all salad ingredients in a large salad bowl.

Dressing: Whisk all dressing ingredients in a small bowl until blended. Pour dressing over salad and toss until coated. Serve on individual salad plates. Refrigerate leftovers.

Makes 4 servings.

ROTISSERIE CHICKEN SALAD

Rotisserie chicken makes this an easy salad to prepare.

**2 cups cubed or shredded cooked chicken from
  a rotisserie chicken**
½ cup sliced almonds, roasted
⅓ cup chopped celery
¼ cup dried raspberries
¼ cup dried cherries

1 6-ounce container low-fat plain yogurt
2 tablespoons mayonnaise
1 tablespoon fresh lemon juice
2 teaspoons Dijon-style mustard
¼ teaspoon poultry seasoning
salt and pepper to taste

Place chicken in a medium bowl. Add almonds, celery and dried fruit.

Stir remaining ingredients in a small bowl until blended. Add to chicken mixture.
Toss lightly. Serve or refrigerate. Refrigerate leftovers.

Makes 4 servings.

SALMON RASPBERRY SALAD

Serve this luncheon salad with hard rolls and iced tea.

4 salmon fillets, rinsed and patted dry
1¼ cups balsamic vinaigrette, divided

8 cups spring mix salad greens
1 cup fresh raspberries, rinsed and patted dry
½ cup toasted chopped walnuts

Brush salmon with ¼ cup vinaigrette. Place on a grill over medium heat and cook about 5 minutes per side or until salmon reaches an internal temperature of 150° and flakes easily. Remove from grill.

Divide salad greens equally among 4 salad plates. Top each with equal portions of raspberries and walnuts. Place a cooked fillet over salad and drizzle each with ¼ cup vinaigrette. Serve. Refrigerate leftovers.

Makes 4 servings.

TURKEY SALAD

Now you have a choice for that leftover turkey . . . a delightful salad.

1 bunch hearts of romaine greens
½ cup bleu cheese, crumbled
12 kalamata olives
2 cups cooked turkey, cubed
½ cup walnuts
½ cup plain croutons
⅓ cup dried raspberries
1 green or yellow apple, cored and sliced
½ cup sliced red onion

Italian vinaigrette salad dressing

Mix all ingredients except salad dressing in a large salad bowl. Drizzle with dressing. Toss. Refrigerate leftovers.

Makes 4 servings.

ARUGULA RASPBERRY SALAD

Crumbled goat cheese and fresh raspberries complement this salad.

3 5-ounce bags baby arugula blend salad greens
1½ cups raspberry vinaigrette (bottled or prepared)

2 6-ounce containers fresh raspberries, rinsed and patted dry
1½ cups crumbled goat cheese (8 ounces)

Mix salad greens and vinaigrette in a large salad bowl. Place equal portions on 12 individual salad plates. Top each with raspberries and cheese. Refrigerate leftovers.

Makes 12 servings.

AVOCADO, MANGO AND RASPBERRY SALAD

A delightful fruit and nut salad.

Dressing
½ cup fresh raspberries
¼ cup extra virgin olive oil
¼ cup red wine vinegar
1 clove garlic, coarsely chopped
¼ teaspoon salt
⅛ teaspoon freshly ground black pepper

Salad
8 cups mixed salad greens
1 ripe avocado, peeled, pitted and diced
1 ripe mango, peeled, pitted and diced
½ cup thinly sliced red onion
¼ cup toasted chopped hazelnuts or sliced almonds
1 cup fresh raspberries, rinsed and patted dry

Dressing: Puree ½ cup raspberries, olive oil, vinegar, garlic, salt and black pepper in a blender; set aside.

Salad: Mix all salad ingredients except raspberries and nuts in a large bowl. Add dressing; toss. Place the salad on 4 individual salad plates. Top each equally with raspberries and nuts. Serve. Refrigerate leftovers.

Makes 4 servings.

BEET SPINACH RASPBERRY SALAD

Fresh raspberries and beets are the stars in this spinach salad.

1 large beet, cooked, cooled, peeled and cut into strips
6 cups baby spinach
¼ cup sliced green onion
¼ cup glazed walnuts

¼ cup extra virgin olive oil
¼ cup raspberry vinegar
1 tablespoon honey
2 teaspoons Dijon-style mustard
¼ teaspoon salt
freshly ground black pepper to taste

1 6-ounce container fresh raspberries, rinsed and patted dry

Mix beets, spinach, green onions and walnuts in a large salad bowl.

Dressing: Whisk olive oil, vinegar, honey, mustard, salt and pepper in a small bowl.

Pour dressing over salad. Toss to coat. Sprinkle with raspberries. Serve.
Refrigerate leftovers.

Makes 6 servings.

FRUITED BLEU CHEESE COLESLAW

Great side to serve with those grilled burgers.

1 cup mayonnaise
¼ cup prepared Dijon-style mustard
⅓ cup crumbled bleu cheese
2 tablespoons granulated sugar
2 tablespoons cider vinegar

1 16-ounce package coleslaw (shredded cabbage)
2 cups seedless red grapes, halved
⅓ cup dried raspberries
salt and pepper to taste

Place first five ingredients in a large bowl; whisk to blend.

Add remaining ingredients; mix well and chill until ready to serve.
Refrigerate leftovers.

Makes 6 servings.

FRUITED SLAW

Serve this tasty side with fried fish or on a turkey burger!

4 cups shredded green cabbage
2 cups shredded carrots
1 cup shredded red cabbage
1 cup well-drained, crushed juice-packed pineapple
¼ cup dried raspberries
½ cup mayonnaise
3 tablespoons honey
1 tablespoon cider vinegar

Mix all ingredients in a medium bowl until well blended.
Refrigerate and chill slightly before serving. Store in the refrigerator.

Makes 6 servings.

BOUNTIFUL FRUIT SALAD

Perfect for the brunch buffet, or serve the gang this fabulous fruit salad with their favorite sandwiches for a light supper.

¼ **cup seedless raspberry jam**
2 **tablespoons fresh lemon juice**
2 **cups strawberries, stems removed, halved**
1 **cup stoned, fresh plum wedges**

2 **cups pineapple chunks**
2 **cups cantaloupe chunks**
2 **cups honeydew chunks**
2 **cups nectarine chunks**
1 **cup fresh raspberries**
1 **cup green grapes**
1 **cup whole natural almonds, roasted**

Stir jam and lemon juice in a large glass salad bowl. Add strawberries and plum wedges; cover and let stand up to 2 hours.

When serving, fold in remaining ingredients. Refrigerate leftovers.

Makes 12 servings.

FOUR FRUIT CHEESE SALAD

Simple and delicious.

4 kiwi fruit, peeled and sliced
2 red delicious apples, diced
1½ cups seedless grapes
1 cup fresh raspberries
1½ cups (6 ounces) four cheese Mexican shredded cheese

2 tablespoons honey
1 tablespoon fresh lime juice
red leaf lettuce leaves

Mix first five ingredients in a large salad bowl.

Mix honey and lime juice in a small bowl. Add to fruit mixture. Toss gently and serve on lettuce leaves. Refrigerate leftovers.

Makes 6 servings.

BLUEBERRY RASPBERRY SALAD
IN EDIBLE PARMESAN BOWLS

Fresh raspberries and blueberries tossed with Parmesan cheese, almonds and romaine hearts, served in an edible Parmesan bowl.

Parmesan Bowls
1¼ cups (5 ounces) artisan blends shredded Parmesan cheese

Salad
1 10-ounce bag hearts of romaine lettuce
6 ounces fresh blueberries, rinsed and patted dry
6 ounces fresh raspberries, rinsed and patted dry
2 ounces sliced almonds
½ cup raspberry vinaigrette or to taste
1 cup shredded Parmesan cheese

Preheat oven to 400°.

Parmesan Bowls: Turn four small 6-ounce custard baking cups or four 3-inch diameter drinking glasses upside down. Place on top of the oven or on a table.

Coat a large baking sheet with cooking spray. Spread heaping ⅓ cup cheese into four 6-inch circles on baking sheet, spacing the circles 1 inch apart. Bake 9–10 minutes or until cheese is melted and golden brown. When cheese has melted, remove from oven and immediately use a large spatula to drape each circle of cheese over the cups/drinking glasses, pressing lightly with a potholder to form a bowl shape. Let stand until cool, then remove bowls from cups.

Salad: Mix all salad ingredients in a large bowl. Serve salad in Parmesan bowls. Refrigerate leftovers.

Makes 4 servings.

HOLIDAY GREEN SALAD

Great salad for the holidays . . . but enjoy it on other days too.

Dressing
1 cup fresh raspberries
⅓ cup balsamic vinegar
⅔ cup extra virgin olive oil

Salad
10 cups mesclun greens
2 medium fennel bulbs, thinly sliced
1½ cups dried cranberries
½ cup dried raspberries

5 oranges, peeled and separated into segments
1 cup spiced pecans

Dressing: Process all dressing ingredients in a blender until smooth.

Salad: Mix mesclun greens, fennel, cranberries and raspberries in a large salad bowl. Add oranges; set aside until ready to serve.

Just before serving, add the spiced pecans and toss with just enough raspberry dressing to lightly coat the salad greens. Serve immediately. Refrigerate leftovers.

Makes 10 servings.

Variation: Use caramelized walnuts in place of spiced pecans.

PEAR HAZELNUT RASPBERRY SALAD WITH BERRY DRESSING

Serve this delicious luncheon salad with warm rolls or muffins.

Dressing
3 tablespoons extra virgin olive oil
3 tablespoons raspberry vinegar
1½ tablespoons honey
1 tablespoon Dijon-style mustard
¼ teaspoon salt
freshly ground pepper to taste

Salad
4 cups slightly packed spring mix greens
2 ripe pears, cored and sliced
1 cup fresh raspberries, rinsed and patted dry
¼ cup toasted chopped hazelnuts or toasted whole almonds, chopped
2 ounces Brie cheese cut into thin bite-sized strips

Dressing: Whisk all dressing ingredients in a small bowl.

Salad: Place salad greens and pears in a medium bowl; toss with salad dressing until well mixed. Place on four individual salad plates. Sprinkle each with raspberries and hazelnuts. Top each with a few strips of cheese. Serve immediately. Refrigerate leftovers.

Makes 4 servings.

POMEGRANATE RASPBERRY FRUIT SALAD

Hint: Score a fresh pomegranate; place it in a bowl of cold water. Break it open under water to free the arils (seed sacs). Arils will sink to bottom of bowl and membrane will float to top; sieve. Refrigerate or freeze extra arils for another time.

Dressing
½ cup 100% pomegranate juice
4 tablespoons honey
4 tablespoons olive oil
2 tablespoons red wine vinegar
2 tablespoons chopped mint
2 tablespoons plain yogurt

Salad
2 cups mixed salad greens
2 ripe pears, peeled, cored and sliced, tossed in a bowl
   with 1 teaspoon lemon juice
1 cup fresh pineapple chunks
1 cup fresh red raspberries, rinsed and patted dry
1 orange, peeled and sectioned into 8 chunks
1 tablespoon sliced fresh mint
½ cup arils (seed sacs) from fresh pomegranate

Dressing: Mix all dressing ingredients in a medium bowl; whisk until blended. Set aside or refrigerate up to two days before using.

Salad: Arrange greens on 4 individual salad plates. Top each equally with pears, pineapple, raspberries and oranges. Sprinkle with fresh mint and about 2 tablespoons dressing or to taste. Top each with arils and serve immediately. Refrigerate leftovers.

Makes 4 servings.

SAM'S SALAD

Green salad with glazed walnuts, dried raspberries, dried cranberries and bleu cheese . . . like Sam—unforgettable.

1 5-ounce bag spring mix salad greens
¼ cup balsamic or raspberry vinaigrette
¼ cup glazed walnuts
¼ cup dried raspberries
¼ cup dried cranberries

½ cup crumbled bleu cheese

Place salad greens in a large glass salad bowl. Toss with vinaigrette, walnuts, raspberries and cranberries.

Sprinkle with bleu cheese. Serve. Refrigerate leftovers.

Makes 4 servings.

SPINACH RASPBERRY SALAD WITH MACADAMIA NUTS AND CHEESE

Brie, fresh raspberries and macadamia nuts make this a special spinach salad.

1 10-ounce bag spinach, washed and trimmed and patted dry

¼ cup safflower oil
2 tablespoons raspberry vinegar
2 tablespoons seedless raspberry jam
4 green onions, including some tops, minced
¼ teaspoon salt
3 drops red pepper sauce (Tabasco)
⅛ teaspoon ground black pepper

1 6-ounce container fresh raspberries, rinsed and patted dry
1 4-ounce round Brie cut into ¼-inch slices and then diced
1 3½-ounce jar macadamia nuts, coarsely chopped

Tear spinach into bite-sized pieces; set aside.

Mix oil and vinegar in a small bowl; whisk in jam. Stir in onions, salt, pepper sauce and black pepper. Pour mixture into a large salad bowl. Add spinach; toss. Arrange on individual salad plates.

Top each salad equally with raspberries, cheese and macadamia nuts. Serve. Refrigerate leftovers.

Makes 10 servings.

STRAWBERRY RASPBERRY MOZZARELLA SALAD

Balsamic vinegar lends a special flavor to the fresh berries.

Dressing
¼ **cup olive oil**
2 **tablespoons balsamic vinegar**
½ **teaspoon salt**
½ **teaspoon freshly ground black pepper**

Salad
16 **ounces fresh strawberries, rinsed, patted dry,**
   stemmed and sliced
6 **ounces fresh raspberries, rinsed and patted dry**

6 **cups bite-sized heart of romaine lettuce**

6 **ounces part-skim mozzarella cheese, diced**
½ **cup torn fresh basil leaves**

Dressing: Whisk all dressing ingredients in a small bowl.

Salad: Place strawberries and raspberries in a medium bowl; toss with half the dressing and let stand 5 minutes.

Place the lettuce in a large salad bowl; toss with remaining dressing until well coated. Place the lettuce on individual salad plates. Top each salad equally with berries, cheese and basil. Serve. Refrigerate leftovers.

Makes 8 side salads or 4 main luncheon salads.

WALDORF SALAD

Dried cranberries and raspberries give this apple salad a special tang and texture.

4 Fuji apples, cored and cut into ¾-inch chunks
1 cup chopped celery
1 cup chopped toasted walnuts
¾ cup dried cranberries
⅓ cup dried raspberries
½ cup minced red onion

⅔ cup mayonnaise
⅔ cup plain yogurt
2 teaspoons fresh lemon juice

Mix first six ingredients in a medium salad bowl.

Mix mayonnaise, yogurt and lemon juice in a small bowl; spoon into apple mixture. Stir until well coated. Serve. Store in the refrigerator.

Makes 8 servings.

APPLESAUCE RASPBERRY SALAD

Serve this side salad with assorted meat or cheese sandwiches.

2 3-ounce packages raspberry flavored gelatin mix
2 cups boiling water

1 12-ounce package frozen raspberries
2 cups applesauce

12 large marshmallows
1 3-ounce package cream cheese, softened
1 12-ounce container frozen nondairy whipped topping, thawed

Stir raspberry gelatin and boiling water in a large bowl until completely dissolved. Stir in raspberries and applesauce until blended. Pour mixture into a 13x9-inch glass baking dish. Refrigerate and chill until set.

Melt marshmallows and cream cheese in a saucepan. Cool completely. Stir in whipped topping. Spread mixture evenly on top of the set gelatin. Store in the refrigerator.

Makes 10 servings.

CRANBERRY RASPBERRY GELATIN

Serve this tangy red gelatin salad for a special holiday treat.

1 3-ounce package raspberry flavored gelatin dessert mix
1½ cups boiling water

1 cup fresh or unsweetened frozen cranberries
½ cup raspberry jam

1 8-ounce can crushed pineapple, undrained

Mix gelatin and boiling water in a bowl until completely dissolved; pour mixture into a food processor or blender.

Add cranberries and jam; process until cranberries are coarsely chopped. Pour mixture into a glass serving bowl. Stir in pineapple. Refrigerate until set. Store in the refrigerator.

Makes 8 servings.

CRANBERRY RASPBERRY GELATIN SALAD

Great salad for Thanksgiving . . . but any other day too!

Salad

1 6-ounce package raspberry
   flavored gelatin
2 cups boiling water

1 12-ounce package fresh or frozen
   cranberries, thawed if frozen
⅔ cup fresh orange juice

2 cups granulated sugar
1 8-ounce can crushed pineapple
   in juice, drained
1 10-ounce package unsweetened
   frozen raspberries, thawed
1 teaspoon freshly grated orange peel

Topping

1 3-ounce package cream
   cheese, softened
1 cup heavy whipping cream
½ teaspoon pure vanilla extract
1 cup miniature marshmallows

Salad: Stir gelatin in boiling water in a large bowl until completely dissolved.

Mix half of cranberries and ⅓ cup orange juice in a blender or food processor
with a metal blade. Process at high speed until well chopped, about 2 minutes.
Place mixture in a medium bowl. Repeat process with remaining cranberries and
orange juice.

Stir cranberry mixture and all remaining salad ingredients into dissolved gelatin
mixture. Pour into a 13x9-inch glass baking dish. Cover and refrigerate until set,
about 6 hours.

Topping: Beat cream cheese in a medium bowl until creamy. Add whipping cream
and vanilla and beat on high until stiff peaks form. Carefully stir in marshmallows
by hand. Spread over set gelatin. Cover and refrigerate at least one hour before
serving. Cut into squares. Store in the refrigerator.

Makes 12 servings.

CREAMY RASPBERRY GELATIN SALAD

Garnish this pretty gelatin ring salad with fresh raspberries.

1 6-ounce package raspberry gelatin
1½ cups boiling water
2 10-ounce packages frozen sweetened raspberries,
   thawed and drained
2 8-ounce cans crushed pineapple, undrained

1 8-ounce package cream cheese, softened
½ cup dairy sour cream

fresh raspberries, optional

Spray an 8-cup ring mold with cooking spray.

Stir gelatin in boiling water in a medium bowl until dissolved. Stir in raspberries and pineapple. Pour half the mixture into prepared ring mold. Refrigerate until firm, about 30 minutes. Let remaining gelatin mixture stand at room temperature.

Beat cream cheese and sour cream in a mixing bowl on medium speed until smooth. Spread carefully over the gelatin in the mold. Top with remaining gelatin mixture. Refrigerate until firm, about 6 hours. Store in the refrigerator.

Makes 12 servings.

MOOSE'S DIVINE GELATIN SALAD

Serve this divine salad with cold ham and cheese sandwiches or other favorite sandwiches for a delightful lunch. An attractive tasty appetizer.

1 3.5-ounce package lemon flavored gelatin
1 cup boiling water
1½ cups miniature marshmallows
1 8-ounce package cream cheese, softened

1 cup whipping cream
2 tablespoons granulated sugar
½ teaspoon pure vanilla extract
2½ cups drained, crushed pineapple

1 6-ounce package raspberry flavored gelatin
2 cups boiling water
1 16-ounce package frozen raspberries, thawed

Stir lemon gelatin and 1 cup boiling water in a large bowl until completely dissolved. Add marshmallows and cream cheese; beat with an electric mixer until blended.

Whip whipping cream, 2 tablespoons sugar and vanilla extract in a bowl; fold mixture into cream cheese mixture. Fold in pineapple. Pour mixture into a 13x9-inch glass baking dish. Refrigerate until set.

Stir raspberry gelatin and 2 cups boiling water in a medium bowl until completely dissolved. Stir in raspberries; cool completely. Spoon over first layer. Refrigerate until set. Store in the refrigerator.

Makes 10 servings.

RASPBERRY CRANBERRY GELATIN SALAD RING

Salad and relish all in one . . . perfect side to serve with those Thanksgiving turkey sandwiches.

1 6-ounce package raspberry flavored gelatin mix
1½ cups boiling hot water
½ cup ginger ale
juice and grated rind of 1 lemon
1 10-ounce package frozen raspberries
1 10-ounce package frozen cranberry orange relish

1 8-ounce container dairy sour cream

leafy lettuce

Mix gelatin in hot water in a bowl until completely dissolved. Add remaining ingredients except sour cream and lettuce.

Pour half of mixture into a large ring mold; refrigerate until set.

Spread sour cream over the set mixture; refrigerate about one hour. Add remaining mixture and refrigerate 6–8 hours.

Unmold onto leafy lettuce. Store in the refrigerator.

Makes 12 servings.

RASPBERRY PRETZEL GELATIN SALAD

This salad (could also be dessert) is an oldie . . . but so good.

½ cup butter, melted
¾ cup granulated sugar, divided
1½ cups coarsely crushed pretzels

1 8-ounce package cream cheese, softened
1 teaspoon freshly grated lemon peel
½ teaspoon pure vanilla extract
1 12-ounce container nondairy frozen whipped topping, thawed
1 6-ounce packages raspberry flavored gelatin
2 cups boiling water
1 16-ounce package frozen unsweetened raspberries, thawed

Preheat oven to 350°.

Mix butter, ¼ cup sugar and pretzels in a medium bowl. Press mixture into bottom of an ungreased 13x9-inch baking pan. Bake until lightly browned, about 10 minutes; cool.

Beat cream cheese, ½ cup sugar, lemon peel and vanilla extract in a large bowl. Fold in thawed whipped topping. Spread mixture over cooled crust. Refrigerate covered for 2 hours.

Stir raspberry gelatin and boiling water in a bowl until completely dissolved; refrigerate and chill slightly. Fold in raspberries; pour over cheese mixture. Refrigerate until set. Store in the refrigerator.

Makes 12 servings.

TERRI'S HOLIDAY GELATIN SALAD

Pineapple, cranberries, raspberries, apple and nuts in this festive salad . . . any day will be special when you serve this good salad.

1 20-ounce can crushed pineapple, drained; juice reserved
combine reserved juice and enough cold water to measure 3 cups
2 3-ounce packages raspberry flavored gelatin dessert mix
1 16-ounce can whole berry cranberry sauce

1 cup fresh or frozen raspberries
1 small red apple, peeled, cored and chopped
⅔ cup chopped walnuts or pecans

Bring cold water mixture to a boil in a large saucepan. Remove from heat. Stir in gelatin until completely dissolved. Stir in whole berry cranberry sauce until blended. Pour mixture into a large glass serving bowl. Refrigerate and chill until slightly thickened but not set.

Stir in pineapple, raspberries, chopped apple and nuts. Refrigerate until firm, about 4 hours. Refrigerate leftovers.

Makes 12 servings.

TWO LAYER GELATIN SALAD

A sour cream layer separates this raspberry cherry gelatin salad. Garnish with a dab of mayonnaise and place on a bed of mixed lettuces as desired.

1 3-ounce package raspberry flavored gelatin dessert mix
1 cup boiling water
1 10-ounce package frozen sweetened raspberries

1½ cups dairy sour cream

1 3-ounce package cherry flavored gelatin dessert mix
1 cup boiling water
1 20-ounce can crushed pineapple, drained
1 16-ounce can whole berry cranberry sauce

Mix raspberry gelatin and 1 cup boiling water in a bowl until completely dissolved. Stir in raspberries until thawed. Pour mixture into a 13x9-inch glass baking dish. Refrigerate and chill until set.

Spread sour cream evenly on set raspberry gelatin. Refrigerate.

Mix cherry gelatin and 1 cup boiling water in a bowl until completely dissolved. Stir in pineapple and cranberry sauce. Refrigerate until slightly thickened; spoon evenly over sour cream. Chill. Store in the refrigerator. To serve, cut into squares.

Makes 12 servings.

Meals Paired
with Raspberries

BELGIAN WAFFLES WITH FRESH RASPBERRY TOPPING

Belgian waffles are often made with yeast, however these waffles are delicious without the yeast. Serve them for breakfast, lunch or supper . . . buttered, of course.

2 cups all-purpose flour
3 tablespoons granulated sugar
1 tablespoon baking powder
½ teaspoon baking soda
¼ teaspoon salt

1¾ cups whole milk
¼ cup melted butter
2 large eggs

Topping
2 cups fresh raspberries
½ cup granulated sugar

Preheat Belgian waffle iron to medium-high.

Waffles: Whisk flour, 3 tablespoons sugar, baking powder, baking soda and salt in a medium bowl until well blended.

Add milk, butter and eggs, mixing until just combined; let stand for 5 minutes at room temperature.

Brush Belgian waffle iron lightly with butter. Pour in about ¾ cup batter, or follow your waffle iron manufacturer's directions. Cook about 3–5 minutes or until golden brown. Serve immediately or keep waffles warm in a 200° oven. Refrigerate leftovers.

Topping: Stir raspberries and ½ cup sugar in a small saucepan. Simmer over low heat 5 minutes. Serve warm. Refrigerate leftovers.

Serve waffles with softened butter, maple syrup and raspberry topping.

Makes 12 square waffles.

CHOCOLATE PANINI WITH CHOCOLATE RASPBERRY DIPPING SAUCE

Chocolate lovers, this sandwich is for you!

Panini
1 18-inch baguette with flaky crust
8 ounces semi-sweet
  chocolate baking bar
3 tablespoons unsalted butter,
  room temperature

Chocolate Raspberry Dipping Sauce
⅔ cup whipping cream
8 ounces semi-sweet
  chocolate, chopped
4 tablespoons raspberry
  preserves

Panini: Slice bread on the diagonal into slices ½ to ¾-inch thick, there should be at least 20 slices of bread. Break chocolate into ½-ounce squares. Butter one side of each slice of bread with ½ teaspoon butter and make a sandwich, butter side out, using a 1½ pieces of chocolate per each sandwich.

Heat a large heavy skillet or griddle over medium heat. Or use a panini grill, following manufacturer's instructions.

In batches, cook one side of sandwich until golden brown, pressing down with a spatula. Flip the sandwiches and cook the second side until golden brown, about 30 seconds. Keep warm in oven.

Chocolate Raspberry Dipping Sauce: Heat whipping cream in a small saucepan over medium heat until it comes to a simmer. Remove from heat. Add chocolate; let stand 2 minute until softened. Whisk until smooth. Whisk in raspberry preserves. Serve warm.

Serve panini with dipping sauce on the side. Refrigerate leftovers.

Makes 5 servings.

GRILLED CHICKEN WITH RASPBERRY CHIPOTLE SAUCE

Hint: For quicker cooking, microwave the chicken 10 minutes (in a microwave-safe dish) before grilling.

Sauce
1 cup barbecue sauce
1 cup fresh raspberries, mashed
2 teaspoons mashed chipotle peppers in adobo sauce

1 fryer cut into serving pieces
chopped fresh cilantro

Stir barbecue sauce, raspberries and chipotle pepper in a medium bowl; remove half the mixture and set aside.

Rinse chicken pieces and pat dry. Cook chicken on a lightly-oiled grill over medium heat 45–50 minutes, turning and basting often with half the sauce mixture. Discard any leftover basting sauce.

Remove from grill when chicken reaches an internal temperature of 165°. Place chicken on a serving platter; sprinkle with cilantro. Serve with reserved sauce, buttered corn on the cob and warm hard rolls . . . buttered of course.

Makes 6 servings.

OVEN PANCAKE WITH RASPBERRY SAUCE

The pancake, also called a Dutch Baby, will puff up when baking, then sinks down when removed from oven. Top the sauce with a dollop of sweetened whipped cream for that extra treat!

Pancake
3 tablespoons butter
3 large eggs
¾ cup whole milk
½ teaspoon pure vanilla extract
½ cup all-purpose flour
2 tablespoons granulated sugar
⅛ teaspoon salt

Sauce
4 cups fresh or thawed frozen raspberries
¼ cup granulated sugar or to taste

Preheat oven to 425°.

Melt butter in a 10-inch ovenproof heavy frying pan over low heat. Remove from heat.

Beat eggs in a large bowl until light and pale. Beat in milk, vanilla, flour, sugar and salt. Pour batter into prepared frying pan.

Bake until pancake is puffed and lightly browned, about 15–20 minutes. Slice into wedges and serve immediately with raspberry sauce as desired. Refrigerate leftovers.

Sauce: Process raspberries in a food processor or blender until smooth; rub through a fine mesh strainer over a bowl. Discard seeds. Stir in ¼ cup sugar or to taste. Refrigerate leftovers.

Makes 4 servings.

PORK LOIN WITH SPICY SAUCE

A tasty meal family and friends are sure to enjoy.

1 teaspoon salt
1 teaspoon black pepper
1 teaspoon rubbed sage
¼ teaspoon garlic powder

1 4-pound boneless rolled
  pork loin roast

Sauce
1 10-ounce package frozen
  sweetened raspberries, thawed,
  drained and liquid reserved; set
  raspberries aside

1¼ cups granulated sugar
¼ cup white vinegar
¼ teaspoon ground nutmeg
¼ teaspoon ground ginger
¼ teaspoon ground cloves
¼ cup cornstarch
1 tablespoon butter or margarine
½ teaspoon freshly grated
  lemon rind
1 tablespoon fresh lemon juice

Preheat oven to 350°.

Roast: Mix first 4 ingredients in a small bowl; rub all over pork loin. Place roast, fat side up, on a rack in a shallow baking pan. Bake uncovered about one hour and 20 minutes or until meat thermometer inserted in the thickest part reaches 160°. Remove from oven and let rest a few minutes before slicing. Serve with flavored rice, green beans and warm soft rolls. Refrigerate leftovers, including pork and sauce.

Sauce: Add enough water to reserved berry juice to measure ¾ cup. Mix sugar, vinegar, nutmeg, ginger and cloves in a saucepan. Stir in ½ cup water mixture. Bring to a boil; reduce heat; simmer uncovered 10 minutes. Mix cornstarch and ¼ cup water mixture in a cup until smooth. Stir mixture into saucepan; bring to a boil; cook and stir until thickened. Remove from heat; stir in butter, lemon rind, lemon juice and raspberries.

Makes 8 servings.

RASPBERRY CHIPOTLE PORK CHOPS

Serve with a crisp green salad and warm garlic bread.

4 5-ounce boneless pork chops
1 teaspoon garlic salt
¾ cup purchased raspberry chipotle sauce, or homemade, divided

1 cup frozen raspberries, thawed

Heat grill.

Sprinkle pork chops with garlic salt.

Mix 2 tablespoons chipotle sauce and raspberries in a small bowl; set aside.

Place pork chops on grill over medium heat; brush tops of chops with some of remaining sauce. Cover and cook 4 minutes. Turn chops over and brush with remaining sauce. Cook an additional 4–5 minutes or until pork is no longer pink in center.

Serve immediately with reserved raspberry mixture. Refrigerate leftovers.

Makes 4 servings.

SUNRISE GRANOLA

This granola will make any breakfast special!

3 tablespoons brown sugar, packed
3 tablespoons honey
1¼ teaspoons sesame oil
¼ teaspoon ground cinnamon
¼ teaspoon pure vanilla extract
¼ teaspoon pure almond extract

½ cup whole natural almonds
⅓ cup sliced almonds

⅓ cup dried raspberries
⅓ cup dried cranberries
⅓ cup golden raisins

2 cups rolled oats
⅓ cup sesame seeds

Preheat oven to 350°.
Coat a baking sheet with vegetable cooking spray.

Mix sugar, honey, sesame oil, cinnamon and extracts in a heavy 3-quart saucepan.
Stir and cook over low heat just until sugar is dissolved. Remove from heat.

Stir in oats and sesame seeds until coated. Spread mixture evenly on prepared
baking sheet.

Bake 10 minutes. Stir mixture, then sprinkle almonds on top. Bake 10 minutes.
Cool on baking sheet. Spoon mixture into a large bowl. Stir in dried raspberries,
cranberries and raisins. Store granola airtight.

Makes 8 servings.

TURKEY BREAST WITH SAUSAGE AND FRUIT DRESSING

Turkey and dressing . . . a special meal to enjoy any day.

Dressing
12 ounces pork sausage
2 cups dried bread cubes
1 cup pecan halves
½ cup chopped dried apricots
⅓ cup dried raspberries
¼ cup butter, melted
⅓ cup chicken broth
1 cup sliced celery

½ cup chopped yellow onion
½ teaspoon salt
¼ teaspoon dried sage leaves, crushed
⅛ teaspoon freshly ground black pepper

1 bone-in turkey breast (6 pounds)

Preheat oven to 350°.

Dressing: Crumble and cook sausage in a 10-inch skillet until browned, then drain and discard fat. Spoon cooked sausage into a large bowl. Add remaining dressing ingredients to bowl; mix well.

Loosen skin from turkey in neck area large enough to add dressing. Stuff enough dressing to fill area. Secure skin with toothpicks.

Place remaining dressing into a small baking casserole with a cover. Refrigerate until ready to bake. Cover and bake dressing during the last 30 minutes of turkey baking time.

Place turkey breast, breast side up, on a rack in a roasting pan. Brush with 3 tablespoons melted butter.

Bake, basting often, about 2–2½ hours, or until a meat thermometer reaches 175° and the meat is no longer pink. Remove from oven; let rest a few minutes before serving.

Makes 8 servings.

Sides

BRUSSELS SPROUTS WITH PECANS AND DRIED FRUIT

Serve this healthy side dish often.

1 16-ounce package frozen petite baby Brussels sprouts

1 tablespoon extra virgin olive oil
2 teaspoons balsamic vinegar
2 tablespoons finely chopped lightly toasted pecans
2 tablespoons dried raspberries
2 tablespoons dried cranberries
salt and freshly ground black pepper to taste

Cook Brussels sprouts following package directions. When cooked, place into a serving dish.

Mix olive oil, vinegar, pecans and dried fruit in a small bowl. Pour mixture over Brussels sprouts in serving dish. Season with salt and pepper to taste. Serve immediately. Refrigerate leftovers.

Makes 4 servings.

CHERRY RASPBERRY RICE PILAF

Your family will love this flavorful, nutritious side.

2 tablespoons margarine
1 cup chopped yellow onion
1 cup chopped celery

¼ cup dried cherries
¼ cup dried raspberries
½ cup chopped walnuts
1 tablespoon chopped fresh thyme or 1 teaspoon dried
1 tablespoon chopped fresh marjoram or 1 teaspoon dried
½ teaspoon freshly ground black pepper

3 cups cooked rice

Melt margarine in a large nonstick skillet. Add onions and celery; cook and stir until tender, about 5 minutes.

Add cherries, raspberries, walnuts, thyme, marjoram and black pepper; cook and stir 4 minutes.

Add rice; stir and cook until thoroughly heated. Serve. Refrigerate leftovers.

Makes 8 servings.

FRUITED ALMOND COUSCOUS

Couscous is so easy to prepare . . . try this side dish.

2 tablespoons olive oil
1½ cups instant couscous
¼ cup whole natural almonds, toasted and chopped

2 cups boiling water
¼ cup dried raspberries
¼ cup dried currants
¼ cup sliced green onions
½ teaspoon ground cinnamon
½ teaspoon salt

Heat olive oil in a medium skillet over medium-high heat. Add couscous and almonds; cook and stir about 5 minutes or until heated through. Turn off heat; leave mixture in skillet.

Place boiling water in a bowl. Stir in dried fruit, onions, cinnamon and salt. Pour mixture over couscous. Cover skillet with a tight-fitting lid and let sit 20 minutes. Fluff couscous with a fork. Serve. Refrigerate leftovers.

Makes 4 servings.

LOUISIANA FRUITED RICE

Most folks in Louisiana have white rice on a daily basis. Serve this jeweled side dish warm or at room temperature.

1½ tablespoons light olive oil
2 cups long-grain rice
½ teaspoon salt

4 cups hot water

1 large ripe pear, red or green, cored and diced
⅔ cup chopped dried figs
⅓ cup dried raspberries
1 large carrot, peeled and grated
⅔ cup toasted pecan halves

Heat oil in a medium pot over medium heat. Add rice and salt; cook and stir until rice is lightly toasted.

Add hot water; cover and simmer over low heat 15–20 minutes or until rice is almost tender. Remove from heat; let stand covered, 10 minutes or until tender.

Spoon rice onto a large serving platter. Add pears, figs, raspberries, carrots and pecans. Gently toss. Serve. Refrigerate leftovers.

Makes 8 servings.

POMEGRANATE FRUITED
CORNBREAD STUFFING

Variation: Add 2 cups diced cooked ham into the stuffing; mix well.

2 tablespoons olive oil
1 cup chopped dried apricots
1 cup raisins
¼ cup dried raspberries
1 cup chopped celery
½ cup sliced green onions

1 12-ounce package cornbread stuffing mix
1 cup arils (seed sacs) from a fresh pomegranate
½ cup chopped parsley
½ cup butter or margarine, melted
1 egg, lightly beaten
2 to 3 cups chicken broth

Heat olive oil in a large skillet. Sauté apricots, raisins, raspberries, celery and green onions 5 minutes. Spoon mixture into a large bowl.

Add cornbread stuffing mix, pomegranate seed sacs, parsley, melted butter, egg and 2 cups broth. Toss until well mixed. Add more broth for moister stuffing, if desired.

Makes enough stuffing for a 12–20 pound turkey.

To bake separately from turkey, place stuffing into a shallow buttered baking dish and cover with aluminum baking foil. Bake 25 minutes, then uncover and bake 10–15 minutes or until stuffing is golden brown. Serve warm. Refrigerate leftovers.

Makes 12 servings.

See page 63 for tips on removing the arils from a pomegranate.

RUTH'S BAKED SWEET POTATOES WITH SAUCE

My sister, Ruth, and I are sweet potato lovers.

8 small fresh sweet potatoes,
  washed and scrubbed

1½ cups orange juice
1 8-ounce can pineapple chunks
  in juice, undrained, chunks cut up
½ cup raisins
⅓ cup dried red raspberries

3 tablespoons brown sugar,
  packed
2 tablespoons cornstarch
½ teaspoon pure vanilla extract
3 tablespoons cold water

butter or margarine, softened

Preheat oven to 350°.

Pierce sweet potatoes with a fork. Place on a baking sheet. Bake until tender when pierced, about 45 minutes.

Sauce: Mix orange juice, pineapple including juice, raisins, raspberries and brown sugar in a small saucepan. Bring to a simmer over medium heat, stirring frequently. Stir in vanilla.

Mix cornstarch with cold water in a cup until smooth. Slowly add mixture into the fruit mixture, stirring constantly, until sauce bubbles and thickens. Spoon sauce into a serving bowl.

To serve, cut warm baked sweet potato open. Fluff insides with a fork. Top each with a pat of butter, then top each with a spoonful of warm sauce. Serve immediately. Refrigerate leftovers.

Makes 8 servings.

YAM MANGO RASPBERRY CASSEROLE

Yams or sweet potatoes . . . this tasty side dish is sure to please.

**4 pounds yams or sweet potatoes,
peeled and cut into ¼-inch slices**

2 medium ripe, firm mangos, peeled, pitted and diced
¼ cup dried raspberries
¼ cup butter
**¾ cup brown sugar mixed in a cup with 1 teaspoon
ground cinnamon**

¾ cup sliced almonds

Place yams in a large pot fitted with a steamer basket. Steam about 15 minutes or until tender; set aside.

Preheat oven to 350°.
Butter a 13x9-inch glass baking dish.

Place half the yams, half the mangos, half the raspberries and half the butter into prepared baking dish; sprinkle top evenly with half the sugar-cinnamon mixture.

Repeat layers. Bake 20 minutes. Sprinkle top evenly with almonds; bake 20 minutes. Serve warm. Refrigerate leftovers.

Makes 10 servings.

Cakes
Cupcakes
Shortcakes
Coffeecakes
Cheesecakes

CHOCOLATE ANGEL FOOD CAKE WITH RASPBERRY ORANGE SAUCE

Homemade chocolate angel food cake with raspberry sauce . . . great dessert.

Cake
1½ cups granulated sugar, divided
¾ cup sifted cake flour
¼ cup unsweetened cocoa powder
¼ teaspoon salt
12 egg whites
1½ teaspoons cream of tartar
1½ teaspoons pure vanilla extract

Raspberry Orange Sauce
1 10-ounce package frozen
    raspberries in light syrup, thawed
¼ cup granulated sugar
2 tablespoons cornstarch
2 tablespoons fresh orange juice
¼ teaspoon pure vanilla extract

Cake: Sift together ¾ cup granulated sugar with flour, cocoa and salt two times in a medium bowl; set aside.

Beat egg whites in a large mixing bowl on medium speed with an electric mixer until foamy. Add cream of tartar; beat on high speed until soft peaks form. Gradually add remaining ¾ cup granulated sugar, 2 tablespoons at a time, beating until stiff peaks form. Blend in vanilla extract. Sift one-quarter of cocoa mixture at a time over egg white mixture; fold cocoa mixture into batter. Pour batter into an ungreased 10-inch tube pan. Bake 35–40 minutes or until cake springs back when touched with finger. Invert cake pan and allow cake to cool completely before removing from pan.

Raspberry Orange Sauce: Drain raspberries; add enough water to drained liquid to measure ⅔ cup. Mix sugar and cornstarch in a 1-quart saucepan. Stir in ⅔ cup liquid. Stir over medium heat until mixture thickens and boils; boil 1 minute. Stir in berries, orange juice and vanilla. Cool completely. Refrigerate leftover cake and sauce.

Makes 12 servings.

FLOURLESS CHOCOLATE CAKE WITH RASPBERRY SAUCE

Make this dessert for a special occasion.

Cake
**8 1.5-ounce bars dark chocolate,
coarsely chopped**
1½ cup granulated sugar
1½ teaspoons instant coffee granules
¾ cup boiling water
¾ cup butter, softened
6 large eggs, at room temperature
1 teaspoon vanilla extract

Raspberry Sauce
**1 12-ounce bag frozen
unsweetened raspberries**
½ cup granulated sugar
1 tablespoon raspberry liqueur

Garnish
**3 cups sweetened whipped cream
fresh raspberries**

Preheat oven to 350°.
Butter bottom and sides of a 9-inch springform pan. Line with parchment or wax paper.

Cake: Process chocolate, sugar and coffee in a food processor until finely ground. With motor running, pour boiling water through feed tube. Process 15 seconds or until smooth. Add butter; process 5 seconds. Add eggs and vanilla; process 5 seconds or until mixture is smooth and creamy. Spread mixture into prepared baking pan. Bake 55–60 minutes or until edge of cake is puffy and center is just set. Cool in pan on a wire rack 30 minutes. Cover and refrigerate at least 3 hours before serving.

Raspberry Sauce: Cook and stir frozen raspberries and sugar in a medium sauce-pan over medium heat until sugar is dissolved and raspberries are soft. Do not boil. Strain berries through a fine-mesh sieve into a bowl; discard seeds. Stir in liqueur. Refrigerate.

Invert cake onto a serving plate. Peel off paper. Spread sweetened whipped cream over top of cake. To serve, drizzle raspberry sauce onto dessert plates. Slice cake into wedges. Place a wedge on each plate. Garnish with berries. Refrigerate leftovers.

Makes 8 servings.

CHOCOLATE RASPBERRY POUND CAKE WITH RASPBERRY CREAM

Offer a slice of this delicious pound cake for that special time.

Cake
2 cups all-purpose flour
1½ cups granulated sugar
¾ cup unsweetened cocoa powder
1½ teaspoons baking soda
1 teaspoon salt

⅔ cup butter or margarine, softened
1 16-ounce container dairy sour cream
2 eggs
1 teaspoon pure vanilla extract
¾ cup seedless black raspberry
**   preserves, melted and cooled**

Topping:
¼ cup seedless black
**   raspberry preserves**
powdered sugar

Raspberry Cream
1 10-ounce package frozen red
**   raspberries in syrup, thawed**
1 8-ounce container frozen
**   nondairy whipped topping,**
**   thawed**
2 tablespoons raspberry flavored
**   liqueur, optional**

Preheat oven to 350°.
Grease and flour 12-cup fluted tube baking pan.

Cake: Mix first five ingredients in a large mixing bowl. Add butter, sour cream, eggs, vanilla and melted preserves. Beat on medium speed until well blended, about 4 minutes. Pour batter into prepared pan. Bake 50–60 minutes or until a wooden pick inserted in center comes out clean. Cool in pan 10 minutes, then remove from pan and cool on a wire rack

Topping: Melt ¼ cup preserves and brush over warm cake. Sprinkle top of cake lightly with powdered sugar.

Raspberry Cream: Puree raspberries; strain to remove seeds; discard seeds. Place in a bowl and blend with whipped topping and liqueur. Fill the cavity of cake with the mixture when serving. Refrigerate leftovers.

Makes 12 servings.

COCOA ANGEL CAKE WITH
PEACH RASPBERRY SAUCE

Cocoa angel food loaf cake topped with peach raspberry sauce.

Cake
½ cup all-purpose flour
2 tablespoons unsweetened
    cocoa powder, sifted
⅛ teaspoon salt
6 tablespoons granulated sugar

6 egg whites, room temperature
1 teaspoon cream of tartar
½ teaspoon pure almond extract
½ teaspoon pure vanilla extract
½ cup granulated sugar

Sauce
¼ cup fresh orange juice
1 tablespoon corn starch
1 tablespoon granulated sugar
2 fresh peaches, pitted and
    sliced or a 16-ounce can sliced
    peaches, drained
2 cups raspberries
½ teaspoon pure vanilla extract

Preheat oven to 350°.

Cake: Mix flour, cocoa, salt and 6 tablespoons sugar in a bowl; set aside.

Beat egg whites in a large mixing bowl on medium speed until foamy. Add cream of tartar and extracts. Gradually beat in ½ cup sugar on high until stiff, glossy peaks form and sugar dissolves. Fold in flour mixture, one-third at a time. Spoon batter into an ungreased 9x5-inch loaf baking pan. Bake about 25 minutes or until a wooden pick inserted in center comes out clean. Turn pan upside down on a wire rack and cool completely. Remove cake to a cutting board. Slice into 8 slices, using a serrated knife.

Sauce: Mix orange juice, cornstarch and 1 tablespoon sugar in a small saucepan. Bring to a boil. Boil 2 minutes or until thickened. Remove from heat. Stir in peaches, raspberries and ½ teaspoon vanilla. Cool.

Serve sliced cake topped with cooled sauce. Refrigerate leftovers.

Makes 8 servings.

DOUBLE RASPBERRY CAKE

White cake with raspberries in the cake and topping . . . yummy.

1 18.25-ounce package white cake mix
1 3-ounce package raspberry flavored gelatin
1 10-ounce package frozen sweetened raspberries,
thawed, undrained
4 eggs
½ cup corn oil
¼ cup hot water
½ teaspoon pure vanilla extract

Topping
1 12-ounce container frozen nondairy whipped
topping, thawed
1 10-ounce package frozen sweetened raspberries,
thawed and drained

Preheat oven to 350°.
Grease a 13x9-inch baking pan.

Cake: Mix dry cake mix and dry gelatin in a large bowl. Add raspberries, including juice, eggs, corn oil, hot water and vanilla. Beat with an electric mixer until well blended. Pour mixture into prepared pan. Bake 35–40 minutes or until a wooden pick inserted in center comes out clean. Remove from oven. Cool completely in pan on a wire rack.

Topping: In a large bowl, fold thawed whipped topping into thawed drained raspberries. Spread mixture over cooled cake. Refrigerate at least 2 hours before serving. Store in refrigerator.

Makes 15 servings.

INDIVIDUAL MOCHA SOFT CENTER CAKES WITH RASPBERRIES

Little chocolate cakes with soft centers . . . a little more than delicious!
Hint: Prepare batter an hour ahead. Bake just before serving.

Cake
6 tablespoons butter
1 cup semi-sweet chocolate chips
2 teaspoons instant coffee granules

3 eggs
½ cup granulated sugar
2 tablespoons all-purpose flour
1 teaspoon pure vanilla extract

Garnish
sweetened whipped cream
fresh raspberries, rinsed
and patted dry

Preheat oven to 400°.
Grease and lightly flour six glass custard cups. Place on a baking sheet.

Stir butter, chocolate chips and coffee granules in a small saucepan over medium heat, stirring until smooth.

Beat eggs in a small mixing bowl on high speed until slightly thickened and lemon in color. Gradually add sugar and continue beating until fluffy. Add melted chocolate mixture, flour and vanilla extract. Beat on low speed just until mixed.

Divide batter evenly into prepared custard cups. Bake about 9–14 minutes or until tops are puffy and appear crackled, but the centers are still soft. Cool 5 minutes, then loosen cakes with a thin-bladed knife.

Invert cakes onto dessert plates. Serve warm. Garnish with sweetened whipped cream and fresh raspberries, as desired. Refrigerate leftovers.

Makes 6 servings.

LEMON RASPBERRY ANGEL CAKE

Purchased angel food cake with raspberries and lemon filling.

1 15-ounce purchased angel food cake

1 15-ounce can lemon pie filling
**2 6-ounce containers fresh raspberries,
   rinsed and patted dry, divided**

**1 8-ounce container frozen nondairy whipped
   topping, thawed**

To assemble:
Cut cake horizontally to make 3 layers.

Stir pie filling and 1½ containers of raspberries in a medium bowl.

Place one layer of cake on a plate; spread with half of filling mixture. Top with second layer; spread with remaining filling mixture. Top with remaining cake layer. Refrigerate until ready to serve.

When serving, top with thawed whipped topping and remaining fresh raspberries. Refrigerate leftovers.

Makes 10 servings.

MARSHMALLOW RASPBERRY CAKE

Delicious when served warm, but good cold too!

**5 cups fresh raspberries or 2 12-ounce packages
frozen raspberries, thawed and drained
1 cup granulated sugar
1 3-ounce package strawberry flavored gelatin
3 cups miniature marshmallows**

1 18.25-ounce package white cake mix

2 cups frozen nondairy whipped topping, thawed

Preheat oven to 350°.
Grease a 13x9-inch baking pan.

Spread raspberries onto bottom of prepared pan. Sprinkle evenly with sugar, dry gelatin mix and marshmallows.

Prepare cake mix following package directions. Pour cake batter over marshmallows.

Bake about 1 hour or until a wooden pick inserted in center comes out clean. Remove from oven. Cool in pan on a wire rack.

Serve with whipped topping. Refrigerate leftovers.

Makes 16 servings.

MOLTEN CHOCOLATE LAVA CAKES

Treat your guests with this special dessert.

1 8-ounce bittersweet chocolate
   baking bar, coarsely chopped
¾ cup butter

3 eggs
3 egg yolks
⅓ cup granulated sugar
1 teaspoon pure vanilla extract

1 tablespoon all-purpose flour

Topping
sweetened whipped cream
fresh raspberries
fresh mint leaves

Preheat oven to 425°.
Butter six 8-ounce ramekins; place in a 15x10x1-inch baking pan.

Stir chocolate and ¾ cup butter in a small heavy saucepan over low heat until melted; set aside.

Beat eggs, egg yolks, granulated sugar and vanilla extract in a large mixing bowl on high speed 8 minutes or until thick and lemon color.

Fold in one-third of chocolate mixture. Fold in remaining chocolate mixture and flour. Spoon batter equally into each prepared ramekin.

Bake about 12 minutes or until cake edges feel firm. Cool in ramekins on a wire rack 3 minutes. Use a knife to loosen cakes from sides of ramekins. Invert onto dessert plates. Serve immediately.

Top each serving with sweetened whipped cream. Garnish with fresh raspberries and fresh mint. Refrigerate leftovers.

Makes 6 servings.

RASPBERRY POKE CAKE WITH CREAM AND BERRIES

Variation: Use thawed whipped topping in place of whipped cream.

Cake
1 18.25-ounce package white cake mix
1 3-ounce package raspberry flavored gelatin
1 cup boiling water
½ cup cold water

Topping
1½ cups whipping cream
2 tablespoons granulated sugar
1 teaspoon pure vanilla extract
fresh raspberries, rinsed and patted dry

Preheat oven to 350°.

Cake: Prepare and cool cake as directed on package for a 13x9-inch baking pan. When cool, pierce top with a fork over entire cake.

Stir gelatin and boiling water in a small bowl until completely dissolved. Stir in cold water. Pour mixture over pierced cake. Refrigerate 2 hours.

Topping: Beat cream and granulated sugar in a medium bowl on medium speed 1 minute. Add vanilla; beat on high speed until soft peaks form.

Serve cake topped with a dollop of whipped cream and fresh raspberries as desired. Refrigerate leftovers.

Makes 12 servings.

RASPBERRY TEA CAKE WITH CREAMY FILLING

Creamy mascarpone filling is the star in this raspberry tea cake.

Cake
2 cups all-purpose flour
2 teaspoons baking powder
½ teaspoon baking soda
½ teaspoon salt
½ cup butter, softened
1 cup granulated sugar
2 large eggs
1 teaspoon pure vanilla extract

½ teaspoon pure almond extract
¾ cup dairy sour cream
1 cup fresh raspberries

Filling
1½ cups whipping cream
⅔ cup granulated sugar, divided
8 ounces mascarpone cheese
1 teaspoon pure vanilla extract

Preheat oven to 350°.
Grease a 9x5-inch loaf baking pan.

Cake: Mix flour, baking powder, baking soda and salt in a bowl; set aside. Beat butter and sugar in a mixing bowl on medium speed until fluffy. Beat in eggs and extracts. Gradually beat in dry ingredients on low speed, alternating with sour cream. Fold in raspberries by hand. Spoon batter into prepared pan. Bake 50–60 minutes or until a wooden pick inserted in center comes out clean. Cool in pan 10 minutes, then remove from pan and cool completely on a wire rack.

Filling: Beat whipping cream and ⅓ cup sugar to stiff peaks in a large bowl. Beat cheese and ⅓ cup sugar and vanilla in another bowl until creamy. Fold mixture into whipped cream mixture.

Slice the cooled cake with a serrated knife lengthwise into 4 layers. Place one layer on a plate. Top with filling. Top with another layer of cake, then top with filling. Add another cake layer and top with filling, ending with one unfilled layer on top. Sprinkle with powdered sugar. Cover and store in the refrigerator. Cut into individual serving pieces.

Makes 8 servings.

RED VELVET CAKE WITH CREAM CHEESE AND BERRIES

A creamy frosting topped with fresh berries makes this a tasty cake.

2¼ cups cake flour
½ cup unsweetened cocoa powder
1 teaspoon baking soda
½ teaspoon salt
1½ cups granulated sugar
¾ cup butter, softened
1 1-ounce bottle red food coloring
2 eggs
2 teaspoons pure vanilla extract
1 cup buttermilk
1 teaspoon white vinegar

Frosting
1 8-ounce package cream cheese, softened
¼ cup butter, softened
1 teaspoon pure vanilla extract
1¼ cups powdered sugar
1 half-pint fresh raspberries, rinsed and dried
1 half-pint fresh blueberries, rinsed and dried

Preheat oven to 350°.
Grease a 13x9-inch baking pan.

Cake: Mix cake flour, cocoa powder, baking soda and salt in a medium bowl until well blended; set aside. Beat 1½ cups sugar and ¾ cup butter in a large mixing bowl on medium speed until creamy. Beat in food coloring, eggs and vanilla. Gradually beat in flour mixture alternately with buttermilk and vinegar until well mixed. Pour batter into prepared pan.

Bake 35–40 minutes or until a wooden pick inserted in center comes out clean. Cool in pan 10 minutes. Remove from pan. Cool completely.

Frosting: Beat cream cheese and butter in a medium bowl until smooth. Beat in vanilla and powdered sugar until smooth. Spread frosting on cooled cake. Press berries gently into frosting. Store in refrigerator.

Makes 15 servings.

RHUBARB RASPBERRY DUMP CAKE

A dump cake dessert is delicious and so easy to prepare.

6 cups fresh rhubarb cut into 1-inch pieces
2 cups fresh raspberries
1½ cups granulated sugar
1 6-ounce package raspberry flavored gelatin
1 18-ounce package white cake mix
1 cup chopped walnuts or pecans
1 cup cold water
½ cup butter or margarine, melted

Preheat oven to 350°.
Grease a 13x9-inch glass baking dish.

Spread rhubarb evenly onto bottom of prepared baking dish. Top evenly with raspberries. Sprinkle with sugar. Sprinkle with dry gelatin. Sprinkle with dry cake mix. Sprinkle with walnuts. Carefully pour water over top. Drizzle evenly with melted butter.

Bake about 40–45 minutes.

Serve warm in dessert bowls topped with vanilla ice cream or serve cold with whipped topping. Refrigerate leftovers.

Makes 10 servings.

Variation: Use thawed frozen rhubarb and raspberries.

DOUBLE RASPBERRY CREAM FILLED CUPCAKES

Pretty pink creamy cupcakes . . . a delicious treat.

Cupcakes
1 8-ounce package cream cheese, softened
½ cup butter
1¼ cups granulated sugar
2 eggs
¼ cup whole milk
1 teaspoon pure vanilla extract
2 cups all-purpose flour
1 teaspoon baking powder
½ teaspoon baking soda
¼ teaspoon salt

Filling
1 8-ounce package cream cheese, softened
1 egg
3 tablespoons fresh or thawed frozen raspberries
⅓ cup granulated sugar

Frosting
3 cups powdered sugar
¼ cup butter
2 tablespoons raspberry jam
1 teaspoon pure vanilla extract
1 to 3 tablespoons whole milk, or as needed

Preheat oven to 350°. Paper line muffin pan.

Cupcakes: Beat cream cheese, butter and sugar in a mixing bowl. Beat in eggs, milk and extract. Stir in remaining ingredients (batter will be stiff). Fill cups ½ full with batter. Make an indentation in center of each.

Filling: Beat all filling ingredients in a mixing bowl until well mixed. Add 2 teaspoonfuls to the indentation of each cupcake. Bake about 25–30 minutes or until test done. Cool in pan 10 minutes. Remove warm cakes from pan; cool on a wire rack. Frost cooled cupcakes. Refrigerate until ready to use. Store leftovers in the refrigerator.

Frosting: Beat all ingredients except milk in a medium mixing bowl. Gradually add milk until frosting is creamy. Refrigerate leftovers.

Makes 27 cupcakes.

LEMON SPONGE CUPCAKES WITH FRESH BERRIES AND CREAM

Raspberries and blueberries top these special cupcakes.

⅓ cup whole milk
¼ cup butter, room temperature

⅔ cup granulated sugar
2 eggs, separated
1 teaspoon lemon extract

1 cup all-purpose flour
1 teaspoon baking soda
¼ teaspoon salt
sweetened whipped cream
fresh raspberries and blueberries,
    rinsed and dried

Preheat oven to 350°.
Paper line 10 muffin cups.

Scald milk and butter together in a small saucepan. Remove from heat and let cool slightly.

Beat sugar, egg yolks and extract with a whisk in a medium bowl. Slowly whisk in milk mixture. Add flour, baking soda and salt; mix well.

Beat egg whites in another bowl until stiff peaks form; gently fold into batter. Spoon batter into prepared muffin cups.

Bake about 15 minutes or until a wooden pick inserted in center comes out clean. Remove from cups while slightly warm, then cool completely.

Serve topped with whipped cream and fresh berries. Refrigerate leftovers.

Makes 10 cupcakes.

PEANUT BUTTER & JELLY CUPCAKES

A cake mix is used in this cupcake recipe.

1 18.25-ounce package yellow cake mix (the kind without pudding)
1 cup creamy peanut butter
½ cup raspberry jelly

Frosting
½ cup butter
1 cup brown sugar, packed
¼ cup whole milk (approximate)
1 teaspoon pure vanilla extract
2 cups powdered sugar

Preheat oven to 350°.
Paper line a 24-cup muffin pan.

Cupcakes: Beat cake mix and peanut butter in a large bowl with an electric mixer on medium speed until coarse crumbs form. Continue preparing cake mix according to package directions, omitting oil.

Spoon batter evenly into prepared pan, filling each only half full. Top each with 1 teaspoon jelly, then carefully top with remaining batter.

Bake 20 minutes or until a wooden pick inserted in centers comes out clean. Cool 10 minutes in pan. Remove from pan; cool completely on a wire rack. Spread with frosting as desired. Refrigerate leftovers.

Frosting: Melt butter in a 2-quart saucepan over medium heat. Stir in brown sugar. Bring mixture to a boil, stirring constantly. Reduce heat to low; boil and stir 2 minutes. Remove from heat. Stir in milk and vanilla. Gradually stir in powdered sugar. Beat until smooth. Add more milk, a little at a time, if frosting is too thick. Add more sugar if too thin.

Makes 24 cupcakes.

HOMEMADE SHORTCAKES WITH BERRIES AND CREAM

You can taste the homemade goodness in this dessert.

Shortcakes
1¼ cups all-purpose flour
¾ cup granulated sugar
2½ teaspoons baking powder
½ teaspoon salt

⅓ cup butter, softened
2 eggs
1¼ teaspoons pure vanilla extract
⅔ cup whole milk

Topping
1 cup fresh raspberries
1 cup fresh strawberries, halved
1 cup fresh blueberries
sweetened whipped cream

Preheat oven to 400°.
Grease and flour an 8x8-inch square baking pan.

Shortcakes: Mix flour, sugar, baking powder and salt in a medium mixing bowl until blended.

Add butter, eggs, vanilla extract and milk. Beat on medium speed until well blended, about 3 minutes. Pour mixture into prepared baking pan. Bake about 25–28 minutes until lightly browned. Cool completely in pan. Cut into squares.

When serving, top shortcakes with sweetened whipped cream and fresh berries as desired. Refrigerate leftovers.

Makes 6 servings.

Variation: Use frozen berries, thawed.

PEACHES, BERRIES 'N ICE CREAM SHORTCAKES

Variation: Vanilla raspberry frozen yogurt in place of ice cream.

Filling
2 cups fresh raspberries
⅓ cup granulated sugar
2 fresh peaches, peeled and sliced

½ cup seedless raspberry jam, warmed
3 cups vanilla ice cream, slightly softened

Shortcakes
2 cups all-purpose flour
½ cup granulated sugar
1 tablespoon baking powder
¼ teaspoon salt
½ cup butter or margarine
½ cup white vanilla chips
⅔ cup milk
¼ teaspoon pure almond extract
1 tablespoon granulated sugar
¼ cup sliced almonds

Preheat oven to 400°.
Spray a baking sheet with nonstick cooking spray.

Filling: Mix raspberries and ⅓ cup sugar in a medium bowl; crush a few berries. Let stand a few minutes. Add peaches; stir gently. Set aside.

Shortcakes: Mix flour, ½ cup sugar, baking powder and salt in a large bowl. Cut in butter with a pastry blender or fork until coarse crumbs form. Stir in vanilla chips. Add milk and almond extract; stir dough until dough is moistened. Drop dough by heaping tablespoonfuls onto prepared baking sheet, making 6 shortcakes. Sprinkle tops with 1 tablespoon sugar. Top with sliced almonds. Bake about 12–14 minutes and firm to touch.

To serve, split warm shortcakes; place bottom halves on serving plates. Top each with a scoop of ice cream, then with 1 tablespoon warm jam and ½ cup raspberry peach mixture. Top with other half of shortcakes. Serve immediately. Refrigerate leftovers.

Makes 6 servings.

CREAM CHEESE RASPBERRY BRAID

Raspberry and cream cheese . . . so good.

Dough
2¼ teaspoons instant yeast
¼ cup lukewarm water
½ cup lukewarm whole milk
¼ cup butter
1¼ teaspoons salt
¼ cup granulated sugar
1 teaspoon pure vanilla extract

Filling
1 8-ounce package cream cheese,
softened
2 tablespoons butter, softened
¼ cup granulated sugar
⅛ teaspoon salt
1 teaspoon pure vanilla extract
½ cup raspberry jam mixed with
2 tablespoons all-purpose flour
1 egg, slightly beaten

Dough: Combine all the dough ingredients in a large mixing bowl. Mix and knead, by hand or mixer, until soft, smooth dough is formed. Place dough in a lightly greased bowl. Cover and let rise about 55 minutes.

Filling: Beat cream cheese, butter, sugar, salt and vanilla extract in a medium bowl until creamy. Add jam mixture and egg; beat until blended.

Divide dough in half; place on a lightly-oiled surface. Roll each half into a 12x8-inch rectangle. Place rectangles on lightly greased baking sheets. Spread half of the filling lengthwise down the center third of each rectangle. Cut 1-inch-wide strips from each side of the filling out to the edges of the dough. Fold about an inch of dough at each end over filling; then fold the strips at an angle, across filling, alternating from side to side.

Cover braids and let rise until doubled in bulk, about 1½ hours. Mix an egg in a small bowl with 1 tablespoon water; brush lightly on braids. Bake in a preheated 350° oven until golden brown about 35–45 minutes. Remove from oven; cool on a wire rack. Refrigerate leftovers.

Makes 2 braids.

CREAMY ALMOND RASPBERRY
COFFEE CAKE

A cake mix is used in this tasty coffee cake . . . and raspberry preserves run through it!

1 18-ounce package moist white cake mix
¼ cup dairy sour cream
1 teaspoon pure vanilla extract
¼ teaspoon pure almond extract
2 large eggs, divided

1 8-ounce package cream cheese, softened
¼ cup granulated sugar

½ cup raspberry preserves
½ cup sliced almonds

powdered sugar
fresh raspberries,
   rinsed and patted dry

Preheat oven to 350°.
Grease and flour a 9x9-inch baking pan.

Beat dry cake mix, sour cream, extracts and 1 egg in a large mixing bowl on low speed until crumbly. Reserve ½ cup crumb mixture. Press remaining mixture in bottom and 1 inch up sides of prepared pan. Bake until light brown, about 15–20 minutes. Remove from oven.

Beat cream cheese, sugar and 1 egg in a medium mixing bowl on medium speed until creamy. Pour mixture over baked crust.

Drop preserves by teaspoonfuls evenly over cream cheese mixture, but do not stir. Mix ½ cup reserved crumb mixture and almonds in a small bowl; sprinkle evenly over preserves. Return to oven.

Bake 25–30 minutes or until filling is set. Cool in pan 15 minutes before cutting into serving pieces. Sprinkle with powdered sugar and garnish with fresh raspberries. Serve or store covered in the refrigerator.

Makes 12 servings.

114

HOLIDAY STOLLEN

A bread machine makes short work of this fruited coffeecake.

2 large eggs, divided
¼ cup butter or margarine, cut in pieces
¼ cup water (70–80°)
2 tablespoons whole milk
1 teaspoon pure almond extract
½ teaspoon salt
2¼ cups bread flour
¼ cup granulated sugar
½ teaspoon ground cardamom
½ teaspoon freshly grated lemon peel
1 teaspoon ground nutmeg
2 teaspoons bread machine yeast

½ cup slivered almonds, toasted
¼ cup dried raspberries
¼ cup dried blueberries
¼ cup golden raisins
powdered sugar

Measure 1 egg, 1 egg yolk (reserve 1 egg white), butter, water, milk, almond extract, salt, bread flour, sugar, cardamom, lemon peel, nutmeg and undissolved yeast into bread machine pan in the order suggested by manufacturer. Process on dough/manual cycle.

When the cycle is complete, remove dough to a floured surface and knead additional flour, if necessary, to make dough easy to handle. Knead in almonds, raspberries, blueberries and raisins. Roll dough to 12x8-inch oval. Fold dough in half lengthwise, a little off center, so top layer is set back ½ inch from bottom edge; pinch to seal. Place on a greased baking sheet. Cover and let rise until doubled in size, about 30–60 minutes.

Preheat oven to 350°.
Beat reserved egg white; brush on dough. Bake about 30–35 minutes, covering with aluminum baking foil after 20 minutes baking time. Remove from pan. Cool on a wire rack. Sift top with powdered sugar. Refrigerate leftovers.

Makes 1 coffeecake. Yields about 8 servings.

RASPBERRY CREAM CHEESE COFFEECAKE

Raspberry preserves star in this delightful coffeecake.

1 8-ounce package cream cheese, softened
½ cup butter or margarine, softened
1 cup granulated sugar
2 large eggs
¼ cup whole milk
1 teaspoon pure vanilla extract

1¾ cups all-purpose flour
1 teaspoon baking powder
½ teaspoon baking soda
¼ teaspoon salt

½ cup seedless raspberry preserves
3 tablespoons powdered sugar

Preheat oven to 350°.
Grease and flour a 13x9-inch baking pan.

Beat cream cheese, butter and granulated sugar in a mixing bowl on medium speed until creamy. Beat in eggs, milk and vanilla until smooth.

Mix flour, baking powder, baking soda and salt in a small bowl; slowly add to cream cheese mixture and beat on low speed until well blended. Spread batter into prepared pan. Top batter with dollops of preserves, then swirl with a knife.

Bake about 30 minutes or until cake begins to leave sides of pan.

Cool slightly in pan. Sprinkle with powdered sugar. Cut into squares. Store in the refrigerator.

Makes 12 servings.

RASPBERRY STREUSEL COFFEE CAKE

Fresh raspberries may be used in place of frozen.

Cake
¾ cup granulated sugar
¼ cup butter, softened
½ cup whole milk
1 egg
½ teaspoon pure vanilla extract

2 cups all-purpose flour
2 teaspoons baking powder
½ teaspoon salt
½ teaspoon ground nutmeg
1 cup individually frozen raspberries, do not thaw

Streusel
½ cup granulated sugar
⅓ cup all-purpose flour
½ teaspoon ground cinnamon
¼ teaspoon ground nutmeg
¼ cup cold butter

Preheat oven to 375°.
Grease and flour an 8-inch square baking pan.

Cake: Beat ¾ cup sugar and ¼ cup butter in a large mixing bowl on medium speed until creamy. Add milk, egg and vanilla extract; beat until well mixed. Reduce speed to low. Add 2 cups flour, baking powder, salt and ½ teaspoon nutmeg. Beat until well mixed. Stir in raspberries. Pour batter into prepared baking pan.

Streusel: Mix sugar, flour, cinnamon and nutmeg in a small bowl. Cut in butter until coarse crumbs forms. Sprinkle mixture over batter.

Bake 35–40 minutes or until a wooden pick inserted in center comes out clean. Cool in pan. Refrigerate leftovers.

Makes 8 servings.

CHOCOLATE CHEESECAKE WITH RASPBERRY SAUCE

Perfect for holidays . . . for more sauce, just double the sauce recipe.

Crust
1 cup crushed chocolate wafers
2 tablespoons butter, melted

Filling
3 8-ounce packages cream cheese, softened
½ cup granulated sugar mixed with 1 tablespoon cornstarch
2 cups semi-sweet chocolate chips, melted and cooled

½ cup whipping cream
1 teaspoon pure vanilla extract
4 eggs, lightly beaten

Raspberry Sauce
2 tablespoons granulated sugar
2 teaspoons cornstarch
½ cup cran-raspberry juice
1 12-ounce package unsweetened raspberries, thawed

Preheat oven to 325°. Grease a 9-inch springform pan.

Crust: Mix chocolate wafer crumbs and butter in a bowl; press mixture onto bottom of prepared baking pan.

Filling: Beat cream cheese in a large mixing bowl on medium speed until smooth. Beat in sugar-cornstarch mixture. Stir in chocolate, whipping cream and vanilla. Add eggs; beat on low speed just until blended. Pour mixture into prepared crust.

Wrap the springform pan twice with heavy duty foil. Place springform pan in a large baking pan. Add 1 inch of hot water to large baking pan. Bake about 60 minutes or until center is just set. Cool in springform pan on a wire rack 1 hour. Refrigerate. Chill at least 4 hours.

Raspberry Sauce: Mix sugar and cornstarch in a medium saucepan. Stir in cran-raspberry juice until smooth. Bring to a boil. Cook and stir 1 minute. Remove from heat. Stir in raspberries. Cool completely. Serve sauce over sliced cheesecake. Refrigerate leftover cheesecake and sauce.

Makes 12 servings.

CHOCOLATE TRUFFLE CHEESECAKE WITH RASPBERRY SAUCE

Serve this luscious dessert for special occasions.

Crust
1½ cups chocolate wafer crumbs
2 tablespoons granulated sugar
¼ cup butter, melted and slightly cooled

Filling
¼ cup semi-sweet chocolate chips
¼ cup whipping cream
3 8-ounce packages cream cheese, softened
1 cup granulated sugar
⅓ cup unsweetened cocoa powder
3 eggs, lightly beaten
1 teaspoon pure vanilla extract

Topping
1½ cups semi-sweet chocolate chips
¼ cup whipping cream
1 teaspoon pure vanilla extract

Sauce
2 10-ounce packages frozen raspberries in syrup, thawed
1 tablespoon cornstarch

sweetened whipped cream

Preheat oven to 325°. Grease a 9-inch springform pan.

Crust: Mix all crust ingredients in a bowl; press mixture onto bottom and 1½ inches up sides of prepared baking pan. Bake 10 minute. Cool.

Filling: Melt chocolate chips; add whipping cream, stir to blend; set aside. Beat cream cheese and sugar in a large mixing bowl on medium speed until smooth. Beat in cocoa, eggs and vanilla. Stir in reserved chocolate mixture until just blended. Pour mixture into prepared crust. Bake about 50–65 minutes or until center is almost set. Cool in pan on a wire rack.

Topping: Melt chocolate chips. Stir in whipping cream and vanilla until smooth. Spread over cooled cheesecake. Refrigerate.

Sauce: Strain raspberries through a sieve into a 1-quart saucepan; stir in cornstarch; cook, stirring constantly, until thickened. Refrigerate.

When serving, cut cheesecake into wedges. Serve with raspberry sauce and garnish with sweetened whipped cream. Refrigerate leftovers.

Makes 12 servings.

FROZEN RASPBERRY CHEESECAKE

A delicious dessert to fix and freeze ahead of time.

Crust
1 cup vanilla wafer cookie crumbs
½ cup finely chopped macadamia nuts, or pecans
¼ cup butter, melted and cooled

Filling
1 8-ounce package cream cheese, softened
¼ cup granulated sugar
1 teaspoon pure vanilla extract
1 14-ounce can sweetened condensed milk
3 tablespoons fresh lemon juice
3 tablespoons fresh orange juice
1 10-ounce package frozen raspberries in syrup, thawed
1 cup whipping cream, whipped

Topping
2 1-ounce squares semi-sweet baking chocolate
2 teaspoons solid shortening

Preheat oven to 375°.

Crust: Mix all crust ingredients in a bowl. Press mixture onto bottom of a 9-inch springform pan. Bake 7 minutes; cool completely.

Filling: Beat cream cheese and sugar in a large mixing bowl on medium speed until creamy. Add vanilla, sweetened condensed milk, lemon juice and orange juice; beat until smooth. Add raspberries; beat on low speed until well blended. Stir in whipped cream by hand. Pour mixture into prepared crust. Freeze until firm.

For peak flavor, let cheesecake stand at room temperature for 10 minutes.

Topping: Just before serving, melt chocolate and shortening in a small saucepan over low heat; stir to blend. Drizzle over cheesecake when serving. Freeze leftover cheesecake.

Makes 10 servings.

LEMON CHEESECAKE WITH RASPBERRY SAUCE

A lemon cake mix is used for the crust in this cheesecake.

Crust
1 package moist lemon cake mix
½ cup corn oil
⅓ cup finely chopped pecans

Filling
3 8-ounce packages cream cheese, softened
¾ cup granulated sugar
2 tablespoons fresh lemon juice
1 teaspoon freshly grated lemon peel
½ teaspoon pure vanilla extract
3 large eggs

Raspberry Sauce
1 12-ounce package frozen dry pack red raspberries, thawed
⅓ cup granulated sugar

Preheat oven to 350°.
Grease a 10-inch springform pan.

Crust: Stir dry cake mix and corn oil in a large bowl until well mixed. Stir in pecans. Press mixture onto bottom of prepared baking pan. Bake until light golden brown, about 20 minutes. Remove from oven. Increase temperature to 450°.

Filling: Beat cream cheese in a large mixing bowl on low speed until fluffy. Gradually beat in ¾ cup sugar. Beat in lemon juice, lemon peel, vanilla extract and eggs until just blended. Pour mixture into prepared crust. Bake 7 minutes. Reduce temperature to 250° and continue baking 30 minutes or until set. Loosen cake from side of pan with a knife. Cool completely in pan on a wire rack. Refrigerate; chill well before serving.

Raspberry Sauce: Mix raspberries and ⅓ cup sugar in a small saucepan. Bring to a boil; simmer until berries are soft. Strain through a sieve into small bowl; discard seeds. Cool completely. Serve sliced cheesecake topped with sauce and garnished with raspberries. Refrigerate leftovers.

Makes 12 servings.

PECAN CRUSTED COCOA CHEESECAKE WITH SAUCE

Garnish each serving with sweetened whipped cream.

Crust
¾ cup graham cracker crumbs
¾ cup toasted pecans,
    finely chopped
¼ cup light brown sugar, packed
2 tablespoons butter, melted

Filling
3 8-ounce packages cream
    cheese, softened
⅓ cup unsweetened cocoa powder
¼ cup butter or margarine, melted

1 14-ounce can sweetened
    condensed milk
3 eggs
1 tablespoon pure vanilla extract

Raspberry Sauce
1 10-ounce package frozen
    red raspberries in light syrup,
    thawed
¼ cup red raspberry jam
1 tablespoon cornstarch

Preheat oven to 350°.

Crust: Mix all crust ingredients; press onto bottom of a 9-inch springform pan.

Filling: Beat cream cheese in a large mixing bowl until fluffy. Mix cocoa and butter in a small bowl; add to cream cheese mixture. Gradually beat in sweetened condensed milk. Beat in eggs and vanilla until mixture is smooth; pour into prepared crust.

Bake about 1 hour or until set. Cool completely. Remove side of pan. Cover and refrigerate; chill before serving. Store in the refrigerator.

Sauce: Mix all sauce ingredients in a small saucepan. Cook over medium heat, stirring constantly, until thickened and clear. Cool. Store in the refrigerator.

Cut into wedges. Serve with raspberry sauce. Refrigerate leftovers.

Makes 8 servings.

RASPBERRY AMARETTO CHEESECAKE

Raspberry preserves and fresh raspberries top this macaroon cookie-crusted ricotta cheesecake.

Crust
1½ cups (12 cookies) soft coconut macaroon cookie crumbs, processed in a blender

Filling
4 cups light ricotta cheese (30 ounces)
¾ cup granulated sugar
½ cup half-and-half
¼ cup Amaretto liqueur
¼ cup all-purpose flour
¼ teaspoon salt
3 eggs

½ cup seedless red raspberry preserves, heated
⅓ cup toasted sliced almonds
fresh raspberries

Preheat oven to 350°.
Lightly grease bottom and sides of an 8- or 9-inch springform pan.

Crust: Press cookie crumbs evenly onto bottom of prepared pan. Bake 10 minutes. Remove from oven.

Filling: Beat cheese, sugar, half-and-half, liqueur, flour and salt in a large mixing bowl until blended. Beat in eggs, one at a time. Pour mixture over crust. Return to oven and bake about 1 hour or until center is just set. Turn off oven; cool in oven with door propped open 30 minutes. Remove from oven. Loosen cake from rim of pan with metal spatula. Cool completely in pan on a wire rack.

Spread with preserves. Sprinkle around edges with almonds. Refrigerate and chill at least 4 hours before serving. Garnish with raspberries, as desired, when serving. Refrigerate leftovers.

Makes 12 servings.

RASPBERRY RIBBON CHEESECAKE

A ribbon of raspberry runs through it!

Topping
**2 1-ounce squares semi-sweet
  baking chocolate**
¼ cup water
2 tablespoons butter

Crust
**1 9-ounce package chocolate wafer
  cookies, finely crushed**
⅓ cup butter, melted

Filling
**1 10-ounce package frozen
  raspberries, partially thawed**
1 tablespoon cornstarch
**2 8-ounce packages cream
  cheese, softened**
1½ cups granulated sugar
4 eggs
1½ cups dairy sour cream
3 tablespoons cornstarch
1 teaspoon pure vanilla extract

Topping: Cook all topping ingredients in a small saucepan over medium heat until chocolate and butter are melted and smooth.

Crust: Mix crushed cookies and butter in a bowl; press mixture onto bottom of a 9-inch springform pan; set aside.

Filling: Mix raspberries and 1 tablespoon cornstarch in a medium saucepan. Bring to a boil stirring constantly; boil 1 minute. Remove from heat and cool 10 minutes; set aside.

Preheat oven to 325°. Beat cream cheese and sugar in a large mixing bowl on medium speed until creamy. Beat in eggs, one at a time. Add sour cream, 3 table-spoons cornstarch and vanilla; beat until blended. Pour half the batter over crust. Spoon cooled raspberry filling over batter. Top with remaining batter.

Bake about 60 minutes or until just set 2 inches from edge of pan. Turn oven off; leave cheesecake in oven 2 hours. Remove from oven; cool completely in pan. Refrigerate 8 hours. Serve sliced cheesecake drizzled with topping. Refrigerate all leftovers. Makes 12 servings.

WHITE CHOCOLATE CHEESECAKE WITH SPIRITED RASPBERRY SAUCE

Cheesecake with raspberry sauce . . . always a special dessert.

1 cup crushed shortbread cookies
3 tablespoons finely chopped toasted, slivered almonds
¼ cup butter, melted

2 8-ounce packages cream cheese, softened
1 6-ounce package white chocolate baking bars (the kind with cocoa butter listed in ingredients), melted and cooled

⅔ cup granulated sugar
⅔ cup dairy sour cream
1 teaspoon pure vanilla extract
3 eggs

Raspberry Sauce
1 10-ounce jar seedless raspberry preserves
1 cup fresh or frozen red raspberries
1 tablespoon raspberry liqueur

Preheat oven to 350°.
Lightly butter an 8-inch springform pan.

Mix shortbread crumbs, almonds and butter in a bowl; press mixture onto bottom of prepared baking pan; set aside.

Beat cream cheese and cooled chocolate in a mixing bowl on medium speed until blended. Beat in sugar, sour cream and vanilla until fluffy. Beat in eggs, one at a time. Pour mixture into prepared crust. Bake about 50 minutes or until center is nearly set. Cool in pan on a wire rack 15 minutes. Loosen cake from sides with a thin spatula. Cool 30 minutes. Remove side of pan; cool completely. Cover and chill 8 hours.

Raspberry Sauce: Stir raspberry preserves in a small saucepan over low heat until melted. Stir in fresh raspberries; bring to a simmer. Remove from heat. Stir in liqueur. Cover and chill. To serve, cut cheesecake into wedges and drizzle each serving with raspberry sauce as desired. Store cheesecake and sauce in the refrigerator.

Makes 12 servings.

Cobblers
Crisps

CRANBERRY RASPBERRY COBBLER

All-purpose baking mix is used in the topping of this crimson dessert.

Filling
1 16-ounce can whole berry cranberry sauce
1 21-ounce can raspberry pie filling
1 tablespoon cornstarch
½ teaspoon pure vanilla extract

Topping
1½ cups all-purpose baking mix
⅓ cup whole milk
¼ cup dairy sour cream
3 tablespoons granulated sugar, divided
½ teaspoon pure vanilla extract

Preheat oven to 350°.

Filling: Mix cranberry sauce, raspberry filling and cornstarch in a 2-quart saucepan. Bring to a boil over medium heat, stirring occasionally; stir in vanilla extract. Pour mixture into an ungreased 2-quart square baking dish.

Topping: Stir baking mix, milk, sour cream, 2 tablespoons sugar and ½ teaspoon vanilla in a medium bowl until just combined. Drop 9 equal spoonfuls of dough on top of hot filling. Sprinkle with remaining 1 tablespoon sugar.

Bake 25–28 minutes or until golden brown on top and filling is bubbly. Serve warm with vanilla ice cream. Refrigerate leftovers.

Makes 9 servings.

PEACH MELBA COBBLER

A cake mix is used in this easy to prepare peach and raspberry dessert.

8 cups sliced fresh ripe peaches (use canned when not available)
¾ cup granulated sugar
2 tablespoons fresh lemon juice
½ teaspoon pure vanilla extract
1½ tablespoons cornstarch
1 teaspoon ground cinnamon

1 6-ounce container fresh raspberries

1 18-ounce package yellow cake mix
½ cup butter, softened
1 egg yolk

Preheat oven to 375°.
Lightly grease a 13x9-inch baking dish.

Mix first six ingredients in a large bowl until well coated. Spoon mixture into prepared baking dish. Sprinkle evenly with raspberries.

Mix dry cake mix, butter and egg yolk until blended in a medium bowl. Sprinkle mixture over raspberries.

Bake about 45 minutes or until golden brown on top. Cool slightly before serving. Serve with vanilla ice cream. Refrigerate leftovers.

Makes 12 servings.

MIXED BERRY CRISP

Fresh strawberries, raspberries and blueberries are used in this crisp, which is topped with a sugar cookie pecan streusel.

Filling
1 pound fresh strawberries, hulled and cut in half
2 cups fresh raspberries
1 cup fresh blueberries
½ cup peach preserves
2 tablespoons cornstarch
1 teaspoon freshly grated lemon zest
3 tablespoons fresh lemon juice
½ teaspoon pure vanilla extract

Topping
half of 16.5-ounce tube refrigerated sugar cookie dough
½ cup quick oats
½ cup coarsely chopped pecans

Preheat oven to 375°.
Lightly butter an 8-inch square baking dish.

Filling: Mix all filling ingredients in a large bowl until well blended; spoon mixture into prepared baking dish.

Topping: Mix cookie dough and oats in a bowl until just combined. Break mixture into small pieces over fruit mixture. Sprinkle with pecans.

Bake about 40 minutes or until fruit is bubbling and topping is browned (cover topping with aluminum cooking foil if browning too fast). Serve warm, plain or top with vanilla ice cream. Refrigerate leftovers.

Makes 8 servings.

PEAR RASPBERRY CRISP

Substitute 3 large fresh pears, peeled, cored and cut into chunks.

14 pecan shortbread cookies
½ cup sweetened flaked coconut

¼ cup granulated sugar
2 tablespoons cornstarch
½ teaspoon ground nutmeg
1 29-ounce can pear halves, drained and cut into 1-inch pieces
1 12-ounce package unsweetened frozen raspberries, do not thaw
1½ teaspoons fresh lemon zest
1 teaspoon pure vanilla extract

Preheat oven to 375°.
Lightly butter a 2-quart glass baking dish.

Crush cookies in a large plastic food bag with a rolling pin until coarse crumbs form. Add coconut; mix well. Set aside.

Mix sugar, cornstarch and nutmeg in a large bowl. Add pears, raspberries and lemon zest; mix well. Spoon mixture into prepared baking dish. Drizzle with vanilla extract. Sprinkle evenly with cookie mixture.

Bake uncovered about 50 minutes or until bubbly; cover with aluminum foil after 30 minutes baking time. Serve warm or at room temperature with vanilla ice cream.

Makes 8 servings.

RHUBARB RASPBERRY CRISP

Tangy fruit topped with a coconut walnut streusel.

5 cups fresh rhubarb, cut into 1-inch pieces
1 cup fresh raspberries
¾ cup red raspberry preserves
¼ cup granulated sugar
1½ tablespoons cornstarch
1 teaspoon freshly grated lemon peel
1 teaspoon pure vanilla extract
¼ teaspoon cinnamon

1 tablespoon cold butter, cut into pieces

Topping
1 cup coconut
½ cup quick oats
½ cup brown sugar
½ cup chopped walnuts
2 tablespoons softened butter
1 egg

Preheat oven to 375°.
Spray a 9-inch baking dish with nonstick cooking spray.

Mix first eight ingredients in a bowl; spoon into prepared baking dish. Dot with cold butter. Bake 15 minutes. Remove from oven.

Mix all topping ingredients in a bowl. Sprinkle over partially baked mixture. Return to oven and bake 15 minutes. Serve warm with vanilla ice cream or whipped cream. Refrigerate leftovers.

Makes 8 servings.

TRIPLE FRUIT CRISP

Canned fruit is used in this easy to make crisp.

2 14-ounce cans pitted red tart cherries, drained
1 15-ounce can red raspberries, drained
1 14-ounce can wild blueberries, drained
¾ cup 100%-fruit raspberry preserves
2 tablespoons cornstarch
½ teaspoon pure vanilla extract
½ teaspoon pure almond extract

2½ cups low-fat granola with raisins

Preheat oven to 400°.

Stir all ingredients together except granola in a lightly buttered 8-inch baking dish.

Sprinkle top evenly with granola.

Bake about 20 minutes or until very hot and bubbly.

Serve warm topped with a scoop of vanilla ice cream or whipped topping. Refrigerate leftovers.

Makes 8 servings.

Cookies
Bars

LINZER COOKIES

Add this special cookie to your holiday tray.

1 cup butter, softened
¾ cup powdered sugar
1 egg yolk
1¾ cups all-purpose flour
1 teaspoon pure vanilla extract
¾ cup finely chopped blanched almonds

1 egg white, beaten in a small bowl
½ cup slivered almonds
½ cup seedless raspberry preserves

Beat butter, powdered sugar and egg yolk in a large mixing bowl on medium speed until creamy. On low speed, add flour and vanilla extract; beat until well mixed. Stir in chopped almonds by hand. Cover dough and refrigerate 1 hour. Divide dough in half.

Preheat oven to 350°.

Roll out one half of chilled dough at a time on a lightly floured surface to ⅛-inch thickness (leave other half in refrigerator until time to roll out).

Cut dough with a floured 2½-inch cookie cutter. Cut out a 1-inch hole in half of cookies with a floured 1-inch cookie cutter.

Place 1 inch apart onto greased baking sheets. Brush cookies with holes in center with beaten egg white. Top with sliced almonds; press lightly.

Bake 7–10 minutes or until edges are lightly browned. Cool completely.

Spread each cookie without hole with 2 teaspoons preserve, then top with almond-covered cookie and press together lightly. Store in a single layer.

Makes 2 dozen.

RASPBERRY ALMOND MACAROONS

Raspberry butter cream fills this sweet cookie.

¾ cup plus 2 tablespoons ground almonds
1½ cups powdered sugar
3 large egg whites
2 tablespoons granulated sugar

Butter Cream Filling
½ cup butter, room temperature
1 tablespoon powdered sugar
1 tablespoon seedless raspberry jelly
¼ teaspoon pure vanilla extract

Preheat oven to 350°.
Line two baking sheets with parchment paper.

Process ground almonds and 1½ cups powdered sugar in a food processor until very fine. In a medium bowl, whisk egg whites until stiff but not dry. Add granulated sugar, and continue whisking until very stiff. Gently fold one-third almond mixture into egg whites with a rubber spatula, leaving some streaks. Gently fold in remaining almond mixture by thirds.

Use a pastry bag with a star nozzle or make a piping bag for the batter by placing a sturdy plastic food storage bag into a tall water glass, folding its top back around the rim of the glass. Spoon batter gently into plastic bag. Remove bag from glass and close. Snip a hole in one bottom corner. Pipe 1-inch stars onto baking sheets. Bake about 18 minutes or until set but not dried out. Cool completely in pan, then remove from parchment paper. Sandwich cookies together with butter cream. Serve or store airtight for only 2 days.

Butter Cream: Beat butter in a mixing bowl until fluffy. Add remaining butter cream ingredients. Beat until blended. Refrigerate if not using immediately.

Makes 3 dozen.

RASPBERRY SHORTBREAD

Sprinkle with powdered sugar when cool, as desired.

Crust
1½ cups all-purpose flour
½ cup granulated sugar
½ cup butter (not margarine)

Filling
3 tablespoons all-purpose flour
¼ teaspoon salt
¼ teaspoon baking soda
2 eggs
½ cup brown sugar, packed
1 teaspoon pure vanilla extract
⅓ cup seedless raspberry jam
1 cup toasted chopped pecans

Preheat oven to 350°.

Line a 9-inch square baking pan with aluminum baking foil, extending edges over sides.

Crust: Mix 1½ cups flour and granulated sugar in a medium size bowl. Cut in butter with a pastry blender until coarse crumbs form. Press dough evenly onto the foil-lined baking pan. Bake about 20 minutes or until edges are golden. Cool completely on a wire rack.

Filling: Mix 3 tablespoons flour, salt and baking soda in a small bowl; set aside. Beat eggs, brown sugar and vanilla in a small mixing bowl on medium speed. Reduce speed to low. Gradually beat in flour mixture until just blended.

Spread jam evenly over cooled shortbread crust. Pour filling on top; sprinkle with pecans. Bake about 25 minutes or until center is completely set. Cool in pan on a wire rack. Remove foil and cut into 16 squares. Cut each square in half diagonally.

Makes 32 pieces.

RASPBERRY PISTACHIO
CHOCOLATE BISCOTTI

Dried raspberries are used in this delicious crunchy cookie.

3 cups all-purpose flour
2 teaspoons baking powder
½ teaspoon salt

1 cup granulated sugar
3 large eggs
2 tablespoons corn oil
2 teaspoons pure almond extract
½ teaspoon pure vanilla extract

1 cup dried raspberries
¾ cup shelled raw unsalted
   natural pistachios
½ cup chopped high-quality
   white chocolate

8 ounces chopped bittersweet
   chocolate, melted and cooled

Preheat oven to 350°.
Line a large baking sheet with parchment paper.

Mix flour, baking powder and salt in a medium bowl; set aside.

Beat sugar, eggs, corn oil and extracts in a large mixing bowl until blended. Add flour mixture; beat until smooth. Stir in raspberries, pistachios and white chocolate. Drop dough by tablespoonfuls in two 12-inch-long strips on prepared baking sheet, spacing strips 3 inches apart. Shape each strip into 3-inch-wide log. Bake until lightly browned, about 30 minutes. Remove from oven; cool on baking sheet 30 minutes. Remove logs to a cutting board. Line same baking sheet with fresh parchment. Reduce temperature to 325°.

Cut each log crosswise into ½-inch thick slices. Stand cookies upright, spacing about ¼ of an inch apart in 3 rows on prepared baking sheet. Bake about 20 minutes or until light golden. Cool completely on baking sheet.

Line another large baking sheet with parchment paper. Dip one end of each biscotti in melted chocolate; place on baking sheet. Chill until set.

Makes 3 dozen.

THUMBPRINTS

This is a good choice for the cookie exchange . . . if they last that long!

4 cups all-purpose flour
¼ teaspoon salt

1½ cups butter or margarine, softened
1 cup granulated sugar
3 eggs
2 teaspoons pure vanilla extract
1 teaspoon pure almond extract

3 cups toasted chopped pecans
1 cup raspberry preserves

Mix flour and salt in a medium bowl; set aside.

Beat butter and sugar in a large mixing bowl until light and fluffy. Beat in eggs. Beat in extracts. Gradually add flour mixture on low speed just until blended. Cover dough and refrigerate 1 hour.

Preheat oven to 350°.

Spread pecans in a large, shallow pan.

Shape dough into 1-inch balls; roll in pecans to coat. Place balls 2 inches apart on ungreased baking sheets. Make a ¾-inch indentation with your thumb in center of each ball.

Bake 12 minutes. Remove from oven. Press the indentation with back of a teaspoon and fill the indentation with ¼ teaspoon preserves. Return to oven; bake 5 minutes or until edges are golden. Remove from baking sheets; cool on wire racks.

Makes 6½ dozen.

BROWNIE CHEESECAKE RASPBERRY BARS

Brownie dessert bars with raspberry cream topping.

1 19-ounce package brownie mix
1 envelope unflavored gelatin
¼ cup cold water
1 8-ounce package cream cheese, softened
½ cup granulated sugar
1 teaspoon pure vanilla extract
1 12-ounce package frozen raspberries, thawed and drained;
  reserve juice
enough milk and reserved juice to equal one cup
1 cup whipping cream, whipped

Bake brownie mix following package directions for a cake-like brownie in a 13x9-inch baking pan. Cool completely in pan.

Soften gelatin in water; stir over low heat until dissolved. Beat cream cheese, sugar and vanilla in a medium bowl on medium speed until well blended.

Combine gelatin mixture and milk-juice mixture. Mix until blended. Chill until mixture is thickened but not set. Fold in whipped cream and raspberries. Pour mixture over cooled brownies. Chill until firm. Cut into bars. Refrigerate.

Makes 24 bars.

CHOCOLATE RASPBERRY CRUMB BARS

Crumb bars are always a special treat at our house.

2 cups all-purpose flour
½ cup brown sugar, packed
¼ teaspoon salt

1 cup butter, softened

2 cups semi-sweet chocolate chips, divided
1 14-ounce can sweetened condensed milk

½ cup chopped pecans
⅓ cup seedless raspberry jam

Preheat oven to 350°.
Lightly grease a 13x9-inch baking pan.

Mix flour, brown sugar and salt in a medium bowl; set aside.

Beat butter in a large mixing bowl on medium speed until creamy. Add flour mixture; beat until well mixed. Using floured hands, press 1½ cups mixture onto bottom of prepared baking pan, reserving remaining mixture. Bake 10–12 minutes.

Mix 1 cup chocolate chips and condensed milk in a small heavy saucepan. Cook over medium heat, stirring constantly, until smooth. Spread over hot, partially-baked crust.

Stir pecans into reserved crumb mixture; sprinkle over bars. Drop teaspoonfuls of raspberry jam over chocolate and crumb mixture, then sprinkle with remaining chocolate chips.

Bake about 25 minutes or until top is light golden brown and center is set. Cool completely in pan on a wire rack. Cut into bars. Refrigerate leftovers.

Makes 3 dozen.

CHOCOLATE SWIRL RASPBERRY BARS

Made for chocolate lovers! Dust these fudge-raspberry bars with powdered sugar when cool, if desired.

2 cups semi-sweet chocolate chips (12-ounce package)
¾ cup butter

1½ cups granulated sugar
1 tablespoon pure vanilla extract
3 eggs
1½ cups all-purpose flour, mixed with ¼ teaspoon salt

⅓ cup raspberry preserves

Preheat oven to 350°.
Grease a 13x9-inch baking pan.

Melt chocolate chips and butter in a 2-quart saucepan over low heat until smooth. Remove from heat.

Stir in sugar and vanilla. Stir in eggs, one at a time, mixing well after each addition. Stir in flour-salt mixture just until flour is moistened. Spread batter into prepared pan.

Drop spoonfuls of preserves around edges and corners of pan. Gently pull a knife through batter and preserves towards center for a swirled effect, being careful not to over swirl.

Bake about 33–35 minutes until bars just begin to pull away from sides of pan. Cool completely in pan. Cut into bars. Refrigerate leftovers.

Makes 36 bars.

COCOA BROWNIES WITH CHOCOLATE RASPBERRY FROSTING

Frosted brownies are always a welcome treat.

Brownies
4 tablespoons butter, melted
4 tablespoons margarine, melted
1 cup granulated sugar
2 large eggs
1½ teaspoons pure vanilla extract

**½ cup plus 1 tablespoon
    all-purpose flour**
**6 tablespoons unsweetened
    cocoa powder**
¼ teaspoon baking powder

⅛ teaspoon salt
½ cup chopped walnuts

Frosting
½ cup semi-sweet chocolate chips
⅓ cup sour cream
**2 tablespoons seedless
    raspberry preserves**
1 tablespoon light corn syrup
½ teaspoon pure vanilla extract
2 teaspoons butter, softened

Preheat oven to 350°.
Grease a 9x9-inch baking pan.

Brownies: Beat butter, margarine and sugar in a medium mixing bowl on medium speed until creamy. Beat in eggs and vanilla.

Mix flour, cocoa, baking powder and salt in a small bowl; stir into creamed mixture. Stir in walnuts. Spread batter into prepared pan.

Bake 20–25 minutes. Cool.

Frosting: Melt chocolate chips in a double boiler over simmering water; pour into a medium bowl and cool to room temperature. Beat in sour cream, preserves, corn syrup and vanilla on medium speed until fluffy and smooth. Beat in butter. Frost; cut. Refrigerate leftovers.

Makes 16 brownies.

CREAMY LEMON RASPBERRY BARS

A lemon cake mix is the base for these delicious white chocolate, cream cheese bars.

1 18-ounce package moist lemon cake mix
½ cup butter or margarine, softened
2 eggs
¾ cup raspberry preserves

1 8-ounce package cream cheese, softened
2 tablespoons whole milk
1 teaspoon pure vanilla extract

12 ounces white chocolate baking bars, chopped
powdered sugar

Preheat oven to 350°.
Grease bottom of a 15x10x1-inch baking pan.

Mix cake mix, butter and eggs with a spoon in a large bowl until well blended. With floured hands, press mixture evenly into prepared pan. Bake about 20 minutes or until a wooden pick inserted in center comes out clean. Remove from oven; cool in pan 5 minutes. Spread evenly with raspberry preserves.

Beat cream cheese, milk and vanilla in a mixing bowl on medium speed until smooth; set aside.

Melt white chocolate in a saucepan over low heat, stirring constantly. Add warm chocolate to cream cheese mixture; beat on medium speed until creamy. Spread evenly over preserves. Refrigerate and chill until set. Sprinkle with powdered sugar. Cut into bars. Store in the refrigerator.

Makes 46 bars.

CREAMY RASPBERRY OAT BARS

Cream cheese bars with an almond crumb topping.

¾ cup butter
1 cup brown sugar, packed

1½ cups quick-cooking oats, uncooked
1½ cups all-purpose flour
½ teaspoon baking soda
½ teaspoon salt

11 ounces cream cheese, softened
½ cup granulated sugar
2 eggs
1 teaspoon pure vanilla extract
1 18-ounce jar red raspberry preserves

⅓ cup chopped slivered almonds

Preheat oven to 350°.
Grease a 13x9-inch baking pan.

Beat butter and brown sugar in a mixing bowl until creamy.

Mix oats, flour, baking soda and salt in a small bowl; stir mixture into butter mixture until blended. Reserve one-quarter of mixture. Press remaining mixture into prepared baking pan. Bake about 12 minutes or until edges are lightly browned. Remove from oven.

Beat cream cheese and granulated sugar in a mixing bowl. Beat in eggs and vanilla. Spread mixture over partially baked crust. Drop preserves by spoonfuls over cheese mixture; spread evenly.

Mix almonds and reserved oat mixture in a small bowl; sprinkle over preserves.

Bake 25–30 minutes or until set and edges are golden brown. Cool in pan on a wire rack. Cut into bars. Store in the refrigerator.

Makes 2½ dozen.

EASY RASPBERRY BARS

Pretty easy . . . very good.

2 cups all-purpose baking mix
1 cup quick-cooking oats
¾ cup brown sugar, packed
½ cup butter or margarine, softened

1 cup raspberry jam, preserves or spreadable fruit
½ teaspoon pure vanilla extract

Preheat oven to 400°.
Grease a 9x9x2-inch square baking pan.

Mix all-purpose baking mix, oats and brown sugar in a large bowl. Cut in butter with a pastry blender or fork until mixture is crumbly. Press half the mixture onto bottom of prepared baking pan.

Spread with jam over crumbly mixture to within ¼-inch of edges. Drizzle with vanilla extract. Top evenly with remaining crumbly mixture; press gently into jam.

Bake 25–30 minutes or until light brown. Cool in pan on a wire rack. Cut into bars. Refrigerate leftovers.

Makes 24 bars.

RASPBERRY CHEESECAKE BARS

Fresh or frozen raspberries may be used in these good bars.

Crust
½ cup butter, softened
⅓ cup granulated sugar
1½ cups all-purpose flour
¼ teaspoon salt

Filling
3 8-ounce packages cream
  cheese, softened
¾ cup granulated sugar

2 tablespoons cornstarch
3 eggs
½ teaspoon pure vanilla extract
¼ teaspoon almond extract

1 cup raspberries
¼ cup sliced almonds

Preheat oven to 350°.

Crust: Beat butter and sugar in a large bowl on medium speed until creamy. Add flour and salt. Beat on low speed until blended. Press mixture onto bottom of an ungreased 13x9-inch baking pan.

Bake 12–15 minutes or until edges are barely lightly browned. Remove from oven; set aside.

Filling: Beat cream cheese, sugar and cornstarch in a large bowl on medium speed until creamy. Add eggs and extracts; beat until well blended.

Sprinkle raspberries over hot, partially-baked crust. Pour cream cheese mixture over raspberries. Sprinkle with almonds.

Bake 20–25 minutes or until set. Cool completely in pan. Refrigerate at least 2 hours before cutting into bars. Store in refrigerator.

Makes 32 bars.

RASPBERRY COCONUT BARS

A buttery crust, coconut and raspberry preserves in this delicious bar.

1¼ cups all-purpose flour
¼ teaspoon salt
½ cup cold butter or margarine, cut in small pieces
3 tablespoons cold water
½ teaspoon pure vanilla extract

2 eggs
½ cup granulated sugar
1 7-ounce package flake coconut
⅓ cup raspberry preserves

Preheat oven to 425°.

Crust: Mix flour and salt in a small bowl. Cut in butter with a pastry blender until coarse crumbs form. Gradually stir in water and vanilla with a fork until blended. Press dough onto bottom of a very lightly buttered 9-inch square baking pan. Bake about 20 minutes or until lightly browned.

Reduce heat to 350°.

Beat eggs in a small mixing bowl on high speed until frothy. Gradually beat in sugar until thick and lemon colored. Stir in coconut. Spread raspberry preserves over crust to within ¼-inch of edges. Cover with the coconut mixture. Bake about 25 minutes or until golden brown. Remove from oven. Cool completely in pan. Cut into bars. Refrigerate leftovers.

Makes 24 bars.

RASPBERRY LINZER BARS

Sprinkle cooled bars with powdered sugar and cinnamon, if desired.

1¾ cups all-purpose flour
½ cup granulated sugar
½ cup hazelnuts or blanched almonds, ground
1 teaspoon grated lemon peel
½ teaspoon ground cinnamon
¼ teaspoon baking powder
¼ teaspoon salt

½ cup cold butter, cut into small pieces
1 egg, beaten
1 teaspoon pure vanilla extract
½ cup seedless raspberry jam

Preheat oven to 350°.

Mix first seven ingredients in a small mixing bowl. Add butter. Beat on low speed until mixture forms coarse crumbs. Add egg and vanilla; beat until well mixed and dough forms a ball. Divide dough in half.

Press half the dough into an ungreased 8-inch square baking pan. Spread jam on dough to within ½-inch of edge of pan. Roll out other half of dough between two sheets of floured wax paper to an 11x10-inch rectangle. Cut dough into twenty ½-inch strips, starting with the 10-inch side. Place strips diagonally over jam, forming a lattice pattern.

Bake about 26 minutes or until jam is bubbly and edges of crust are lightly brown. Cool completely in pan. Store in refrigerator.

Makes 25 bars.

RASPBERRY OATMEAL BARS

A cake mix is used in this easy bar.

1 18.25-ounce package yellow cake mix
2½ cups quick cooking oats, uncooked
¾ cup margarine, melted

1 cup raspberry jam
½ teaspoon pure vanilla extract
1 tablespoon water

Preheat oven to 375°.
Grease a 13x9-inch baking pan.

Mix dry cake mix, oats and margarine in a large bowl until well blended. Press half of mixture evenly onto bottom of prepared baking pan.

Mix jam, vanilla and water in a small bowl. Spread mixture over crust. Sprinkle remaining cake-oat mixture evenly over top.

Bake about 18–22 minutes or until top is lightly browned. Cool completely in pan on a wire rack. Cut into bars. Refrigerate leftovers.

Makes 24 bars.

RASPBERRY PECAN BARS

Serve these delicious pastry bars for a special event.

2 cups all-purpose flour
½ cup granulated sugar
⅛ teaspoon salt
1 cup butter
1 10-ounce jar raspberry preserves

1½ cups brown sugar, packed
3 eggs
1 teaspoon pure vanilla extract
¼ teaspoon almond extract
1½ cups chopped pecans
¾ cup coconut
4½ tablespoons all-purpose flour
¾ teaspoon baking powder

Preheat oven to 350°.

Mix 2 cups flour, granulated sugar and salt in a medium bowl. Cut in butter with a pastry blender until coarse crumbs form. Press dough in an even layer in an ungreased 10x15-inch jelly roll baking pan. Bake until lightly browned, about 15 minutes. Remove from oven; cool 15 minutes. Spread evenly with raspberry preserves.

Reduce heat to 325°.

Beat brown sugar, eggs and extracts in a large mixing bowl until fluffy. Fold in pecans, coconut, 4½ tablespoons flour and baking powder. Spread mixture over preserves. Bake until center is set, about 30 minutes. Cool on a wire rack. Cut into 1½x2-inch bars. Refrigerate leftovers.

Makes 50 bars.

RASPBERRY PRESERVES BARS

Raspberry preserves fill these buttery pecan bars.

2¼ cups all-purpose flour
1 cup granulated sugar
1 cup chopped pecans
1 cup butter, softened
1 egg

¾ cup raspberry preserves

Preheat oven to 350°.
Grease an 8-inch square baking pan.

Mix and beat first five ingredients in a large bowl on low speed until coarse crumbs form. Reserve 2 cups of crumb mixture; set aside. Press remaining crumb mixture onto bottom of prepared baking pan.

Spread raspberry preserves over crust to within ½-inch of edge. Crumble reserved crumb mixture evenly over preserves.

Bake 40–50 minutes or until lightly browned. Cool completely in pan on a wire rack. Cut into bars. Refrigerate leftovers.

Makes 25 bars.

RED RASPBERRY CHEESECAKE BARS

A good choice when planning a party . . . keeps well.

1 18.25-ounce package moist yellow cake mix
⅓ cup butter, softened
1 egg

3 8-ounce packages cream cheese, softened
¾ cup granulated sugar
3 eggs
1 cup dairy sour cream
2 teaspoons pure vanilla extract

1 21-ounce can royal red raspberry pie filling, chilled
sweetened whipped cream

Preheat oven to 350°.
Grease and flour a 13x9-inch baking pan.

Mix dry cake mix, butter and 1 egg in a large mixing bowl on low speed until crumbly. Press mixture lightly into prepared pan. Bake 15 minutes; remove from oven.

Beat cream cheese in a mixing bowl on medium speed until fluffy. Add sugar, 3 eggs, sour cream and vanilla; beat until smooth. Pour mixture into prepared crust.

Bake 45–55 minutes or until center is set. Cool; then immediately cover and refrigerate. Chill well before serving. Cut into bars.

Top with raspberry pie filling when serving. Garnish with sweetened whipped cream as desired. Refrigerate leftovers.

Makes 15 bars.

Desserts

APPLE RASPBERRY BROWN BETTY

For an extra treat, top with a dollop of sweetened whipped cream or a scoop of vanilla ice cream when serving.

¼ **cup apple juice**
¼ **cup apple jelly**
1 **tablespoon cornstarch**
5 **apples, peelings on, cored and thinly sliced**
⅓ **cup raisins**
1 **cup unsweetened frozen raspberries, thawed**

Topping
¼ **cup rolled oats**
¼ **cup fresh bread crumbs**
2 **tablespoons brown sugar**
1 **tablespoon butter or margarine, melted**
½ **teaspoon ground cinnamon**

Preheat oven to 400°.
Grease an 8-inch square baking dish.

Stir apple juice, jelly and cornstarch in a large saucepan until blended. Stir in apples; cook over medium-high heat until mixture comes to a boil. Cook 1 minute, stirring constantly. Remove from heat; cool. Fold in raisins. Spoon into prepared baking dish. Top evenly with raspberries.

Topping: Mix all topping ingredients in a small bowl. Sprinkle over raspberries. Bake until topping is browned, about 25–30 minutes. Serve warm. Refrigerate leftovers.

Makes 6 servings.

APRICOT RASPBERRY DESSERT

Variation: Use fresh peaches if apricots are not available.

1 package vanilla instant pudding mix (4-serving size)
1¼ cups cold whole milk
1 teaspoon grated lemon peel
1 8-ounce container frozen nondairy whipped topping,
  thawed, divided

1 10.75-ounce frozen pound cake, thawed
  and cut into ¾-inch cubes

1¼ pounds fresh apricots, peeled and sliced (about 4 cups)
2 cups fresh raspberries
¼ cup toasted slivered almonds

Beat pudding mix and milk with a wire whisk in a large bowl until blended, about 2 minutes. Stir in lemon peel. Stir in 2 cups thawed whipped topping; set aside.

Arrange half the cake cubes in bottom of a 2½-quart glass baking dish with straight sides. Spoon half the pudding mixture over cake cubes. Top with half of the fruit. Repeat all layers. Top with remaining whipped topping and toasted almonds. Refrigerate and chill well before serving. Refrigerate leftovers.

Makes 15 servings.

BERRIES AND PUDDING IN MERINGUE

Variation: Use 1 cup blueberries and 1 cup raspberries.

4 egg whites
¼ teaspoon cream of tartar
1 cup granulated sugar

1 package instant vanilla pudding (4-serving size)
1½ cups cold whole milk
1 cup thawed nondairy frozen whipped topping
2 cups fresh raspberries
3 tablespoons powdered sugar

Preheat oven to 225°.
Line a baking sheet with cooking parchment paper.

Beat egg whites and cream of tartar in a medium bowl on high speed until soft peaks form, about 5 minutes. Gradually beat in granulated sugar one tablespoon at a time until stiff peaks form. Spoon onto prepared baking sheet. Make a 10-inch circle of meringue using the back of a large spoon to form a crust. Bake 1½ hours. Remove from oven; cool completely. Place meringue on a serving plate.

Whisk pudding and milk in a large bowl until well blended, about 2 minutes. Stir in whipped topping. Chill 15 minutes. Spoon pudding mixture over meringue, leaving a border of meringue showing around the edges. Spoon raspberries over pudding. Sprinkle berries with powdered sugar. Cut and serve. Refrigerate leftovers.

Makes 12 servings.

BERRY CHEESECAKE PARFAITS

Hint: Store the parfaits in the refrigerator up to 4 hours ahead of serving time.

1 8-ounce package cream cheese, softened
1½ cups cold whole milk mixed with ½ teaspoon pure vanilla extract
1 3.4-ounce package instant vanilla pudding
1½ cups thawed nondairy frozen whipped topping, divided

24 vanilla wafer cookies, coarsely crushed and mixed in a bowl with
   2 tablespoons melted butter and 1 tablespoon granulated sugar

½ cup each: fresh raspberries, blueberries and sliced strawberries
   tossed in a small bowl with a tablespoon of powdered sugar

Beat cream cheese in a mixing bowl until creamy. Gradually beat in milk mixture. Stir in pudding mix until well blended, about 2 minutes. Whisk in 1 cup thawed whipped topping.

Layer half of the vanilla wafer mixture, half the berries and half the pudding mixture into 8 parfait glasses. Repeat. Top each with remaining thawed whipped topping. Serve. Refrigerate leftovers.

Makes 8 servings.

BERRY LEMON TRIFLE

Homemade lemon curd is used in this luscious trifle.

Syrup
½ cup granulated sugar
⅓ cup fresh lemon juice
¼ cup cold water

Curd
4 large eggs
1 cup granulated sugar
⅓ cup fresh lemon juice
½ cup butter, room temperature
1 tablespoon freshly grated
    lemon peel

Topping
4 half-pint containers fresh
    raspberries (frozen raspberries
    may be used)
¼ cup granulated sugar
1 16-ounce frozen pound cake,
    thawed; trim dark outside shell

2 cups whipping cream, whipped
    in a large bowl with 3 tablespoons
    granulated sugar and 1 teaspoon
    pure vanilla extract until peaks
    form

Syrup: Bring sugar, lemon juice and water to a boil in a small saucepan over medium heat, stirring to dissolve sugar. Reduce heat; simmer 1 minute. Remove from heat. Cover and chill.

Curd: Whisk eggs, sugar and lemon juice in a heavy medium saucepan until blended. Stir in butter and lemon peel; cook and stir over medium heat until mixture thickens to a pudding consistency, about 10 minutes. Spoon into a bowl; press plastic wrap onto surface. Chill until cold.

Topping: Mash raspberries coarsely with ¼ cup sugar in a medium bowl; let stand 30 minutes.

Cut cake crosswise into 8 pieces. Cut each piece into 3 strips. Line bottom of a 3-quart trifle bowl with 8 cake strips; trim to fit. Drizzle with 3 tablespoons syrup; spread with ⅔ cup curd and half of the mashed raspberries. Repeat layering. Top with remaining cake, syrup and curd. Spread with whipped cream. Cover; chill well. Refrigerate leftovers.

Makes 10 servings.

BIG AL'S RASPBERRY DESSERT

A scrumptious dessert you can prepare ahead of time.

**10 cream-filled sponge cakes, such as Twinkies,
cut in half lengthwise**
2 10-ounce packages frozen raspberries in syrup, thawed
1 7-ounce package flaked coconut
**1 box vanilla pudding (6-serving size), prepared following
package directions**
1 8-ounce container frozen nondairy whipped topping, thawed

Layer cut sponge cakes in a 13x9-inch glass baking pan.

Top with thawed raspberries. Sprinkle evenly with coconut. Cover with prepared vanilla pudding. Top with thawed whipped topping.

Refrigerate immediately and chill several hours before serving. Store in the refrigerator.

Makes 12 servings.

CHOCOLATE ESPRESSO POTS DE CRÈME WITH RASPBERRY SAUCE

An elegant dessert to serve for special dinners.

2 cups fresh raspberries
2 tablespoons superfine sugar

6 ounces good quality bittersweet
   chocolate, finely chopped
1⅔ cups heavy cream
⅓ cup whole milk

1½ teaspoons instant espresso
   powder
pinch of salt

6 large egg yolks
1 tablespoon granulated sugar
pinch of salt

Sauce: Process 2 cups fresh raspberries with 2 tablespoons superfine sugar in food processor; press through a fine-mesh sieve into a bowl. Discard seeds. Chill.

Preheat oven to 300°.

Place chopped chocolate in glass mixing bowl; set aside.

Custard: Stir cream, milk, espresso powder and salt in a small heavy saucepan. Bring mixture just to a boil, stirring until espresso powder is dissolved. Pour hot mixture over chocolate in bowl, whisking until chocolate is melted and mixture is smooth. Whisk egg yolks, granulated sugar and pinch of salt in another bowl; add chocolate mixture in a slow stream, whisking constantly. Pour mixture through a fine-mesh sieve into a 1-quart glass pitcher. Cool completely, stirring occasionally.

Divide custard among eight 5-ounce ramekins. Cook the custard in a hot water bath. To prepare the hot water bath, pour water into a cake pan. Then place the custards in a separate baking pan lined with a kitchen towel. (This prevents the custard cups from moving.) Wrap the pan with the custards in tin foil. Poke a few holes in the tin foil. Place the pan wrapped in tinfoil into the pan with water. Place the combination in the oven. Cook until custards are set around edges but still slightly jiggly in centers, about 30–35 minutes. Uncover ramekins and cool completely on a rack. Cover and chill well. Top with raspberry sauce when serving. Refrigerate leftovers. Makes 8 servings.

COCONUT RASPBERRY DESSERT

Swirls of raspberry and a creamy mixture in a toasted coconut crust . . . a delicious no-bake dessert.

1 7-ounce package flaked coconut, toasted
⅓ cup butter or margarine, melted

1 10-ounce package frozen red raspberries in syrup, thawed and pureed in a blender until smooth
1 tablespoon cornstarch

1 envelope unflavored gelatin
¼ cup cold water

1 14-ounce can sweetened condensed milk
1 8-ounce container dairy sour cream
2 tablespoons orange juice concentrate, thawed
1 teaspoon pure vanilla extract
1 cup whipping cream, stiffly whipped

To toast coconut, place coconut on a cookie sheet. Bake for 10–15 minutes at 350°, stirring often. Remove from oven and cool before using. Mix coconut and butter in a bowl; press firmly on bottom and up sides of an 8- or 9-inch springform pan. Chill.

Mix raspberry puree and cornstarch in a small saucepan; cook and stir until mixture thickens. Cool to room temperature.

Sprinkle gelatin over water in a small saucepan; let stand 1 minute, then heat over low heat until dissolved; set aside.

Stir sweetened condensed milk, sour cream, orange juice concentrate, vanilla extract and gelatin mixture in a large bowl until well mixed. Fold in whipped cream. Chill until mixture mounds slightly, about 10 minutes. Spread half the mixture into prepared pan. Top with half the raspberry mixture. Repeat layering. Swirl raspberry mixture through cream mixture with a knife or spatula. Refrigerate and chill until set, about 6 hours. Refrigerate leftovers. Makes 10 servings.

COEUR A LA CRÈME WITH RASPBERRY SAUCE

In French, "coeur" means heart. Use other molds if you don't have a heart-shaped mold.

1 cup heavy whipping cream

4 ounces cream cheese, softened
⅓ cup powdered sugar
½ teaspoon pure vanilla extract
½ teaspoon fresh lemon juice
½ teaspoon raspberry flavored liqueur

Sauce
1 10-ounce package frozen raspberries in syrup, thawed
1 teaspoon fresh lemon juice
1 teaspoon raspberry flavored liqueur

fresh raspberries

Line four ½-cup heart-shaped molds with cheesecloth. Place molds in jelly roll pan; set aside.

Beat whipping cream in a mixing bowl on medium speed to soft peaks. Set aside.

Beat cream cheese and powdered sugar in a large mixing bowl on medium speed until smooth. Add vanilla, lemon juice and ½ teaspoon liqueur; beat just until combined. Gently fold in whipped cream. Spoon mixture evenly into prepared molds. Cover with plastic wrap and refrigerate 8 hours.

Sauce: Puree raspberries in blender. Strain through a fine sieve. Stir in lemon juice and 1 teaspoon liqueur. Cover and refrigerate until ready to serve.

To serve, invert molds onto center of serving plates. Remove cheesecloth. Spoon sauce around each heart. Garnish with fresh raspberries as desired. Refrigerate leftovers.

Makes 4 servings.

CREAMY RASPBERRY TRIFLE

Pretty pink color peeking through the creamy cake layers.

1 8-ounce package cream cheese, softened
2 cups whole milk
1 teaspoon pure vanilla extract
1 package vanilla flavored instant pudding mix (4-serving size)
1 8-ounce container frozen nondairy whipped topping, thawed

1 20-ounce can crushed pineapple in juice, undrained
1 12-ounce package unsweetened frozen raspberries, thawed

1 8½-ounce purchased angel food cake, cut into ¾-inch cubes

Beat cream cheese in a large bowl on low speed until smooth. Gradually beat in ½ cup milk until well blended, then add remaining milk, vanilla extract and dry pudding mix. Beat on low speed until blended, about 2 minutes. Stir in whipped topping by hand.

Mix pineapple and raspberries in a medium bowl.

Layer one-third cake cubes in a 3-quart glass serving bowl. Cover with one-third of pudding mixture and one-third of the fruit mixture. Repeat all layers 2 more times. Store in refrigerator.

Makes 10 servings.

HOT RASPBERRY SOUFFLÉ WITH CHOCOLATE SAUCE

Hot soufflé with chocolate sauce and ice cream . . . yummy.

2 6-ounce containers fresh raspberries
3 tablespoons granulated sugar
⅓ cup cornstarch

6 large egg whites
⅔ cup granulated sugar

Sauce
⅓ cup granulated sugar
½ cup water
2 tablespoons light corn syrup
⅓ cup unsweetened cocoa powder, sifted
vanilla ice cream

Preheat oven to 375°.
Butter eight ¾-cup soufflé dishes. Coat with granulated sugar; tap out excess.

Puree raspberries with 3 tablespoons sugar in food processor. Strain into a heavy medium saucepan, pressing on solids. Add cornstarch; whisk to blend. Whisk over medium heat until mixture boils and thickens to the consistency of pudding, about 3 minutes. Transfer raspberry mixture into a large bowl; cool completely. (Can be made 2 hours ahead of time, just cover and let stand at room temperature.)

Beat egg whites with an electric mixer in another large bowl to soft peaks. Gradually add remaining ⅔ cup of sugar, beating until stiff but not dry. Whisk one-third of whites into cooled raspberry mixture to lighten, then fold in remaining whites. Divide mixture among prepared dishes. Bake until puffed and pale golden on top, about 15 minutes.

Sauce: Mix sugar, water and corn syrup in a heavy saucepan; bring to a boil over medium-high heat. Remove from heat. Place cocoa powder in a bowl and add enough of the hot sugar syrup to make a paste, stirring until smooth. Gradually add the remaining syrup; mix until well blended. Serve soufflés, with chocolate sauce and vanilla ice cream, as desired. Refrigerate leftovers.

Makes 8 servings.

INDIVIDUAL BAKED ALASKA
WITH RASPBERRY SAUCE

Pound cake is the base used for this Baked Alaska.

1 11-ounce pound cake
1 pint vanilla ice cream

Meringue
½ cup granulated sugar
2 large egg whites
2 tablespoons water
¼ teaspoon cream of tartar
½ teaspoon pure vanilla extract

Raspberry Sauce
1 10-ounce package frozen red raspberries in syrup, thawed, pureed and strained in a bowl, and mixed with ⅓ cup light corn syrup and ¼ cup fresh orange juice; refrigerate

Cut cake lengthwise to make ½-inch-thick slices. Cut 8 rounds from slices using a 3-inch-round cookie cutter. Place 4 cake rounds on a baking sheet. Top each with a scoop of ice cream. Top ice cream with remaining 4 cake rounds. Press down lightly and scrape away any ice cream that has pressed out of the sides. Cover with plastic wrap and freeze until solid.

Meringue: In top of a double boiler, over simmering water, place sugar, egg whites, water and cream of tartar. Beat with a handheld mixer on low speed 3–5 minutes, until an instant-read thermometer registers 160°, then continue beating on high speed 3 minutes. Remove from heat and beat until cool, about 4 minutes, beating in vanilla when peaks start to form. Cover with plastic wrap; refrigerate 15 minutes.

Preheat the broiler when ready to serve.

Remove cakes from freezer and immediately spread with meringue, sealing cake completely; swirl to make peaks. Place cakes under broiler (still on the baking sheet) as close to the heat as possible, to brown meringue tips, about 1 minute. Serve immediately with raspberry sauce spooned onto individual dessert plates. Freeze leftovers. Makes 4 servings.

Variation: Use rounds of baked brownies or chocolate cake.

KI KI'S RASPBERRY
ANGEL FOOD DESSERT

My friend, Ki Ki, lives in Minnesota and shares this angelic recipe.

1 3-ounce package strawberry flavored gelatin dessert mix
¼ cup boiling water
1 10-ounce package frozen raspberries, thawed
1 tablespoon granulated sugar
pinch of salt

2 cups whipping cream, whipped with 2 tablespoons granulated
   sugar and 1 teaspoon pure vanilla extract

half of a 10-inch prepared angel food cake, torn into pieces

additional sweetened whipped cream
fresh raspberries

Dissolve gelatin in boiling water in a large bowl. Stir in raspberries, including juice. Stir in sugar and salt. Cool until mixture begins to thicken, but is not set. Fold in whipped cream.

Cover bottom of a 9-inch square glass baking dish evenly with cake pieces. Top evenly with half of the raspberry cream mixture.

Make another layer with remaining cake pieces. Pour remaining raspberry cream mixture over top.

Refrigerate until set, about 5 hours. Cut into squares. Serve topped with additional whipped cream and fresh raspberries, as desired. Store in the refrigerator.

Makes 8 servings.

LEMON RICOTTA DESSERT BARS WITH RASPBERRY SAUCE

Ricotta cheesecake bars topped with raspberry sauce.

Raspberry Sauce
**2 12-ounce packages frozen dry
  pack red raspberries**
⅔ cup granulated sugar

Filling
3 eggs, lightly beaten
2 15-ounce containers ricotta cheese
¾ cup granulated sugar
2 teaspoons freshly grated lemon peel

Cake
**1 18-ounce package lemon
  cake mix**
1 cup cold water
⅓ cup corn oil
¼ cup fresh lemon juice
3 eggs

Preheat oven to 350°.
Grease a 13x9-inch baking pan.

Sauce: Mix raspberries and sugar in a medium saucepan. Bring to a boil; simmer until berries are soft. Strain through a sieve into a bowl; discard seeds. Cool completely.

Filling: Mix eggs, ricotta cheese, sugar and lemon peel in a large bowl.

Cake: Beat cake mix, water, corn oil, lemon juice and eggs on low speed 30 seconds. Beat on medium speed 2 minutes. Pour batter into prepared baking pan. Carefully spoon cheese mixture on top; spread evenly.

Bake 60–65 minutes or until lightly browned. Cool in pan on a wire rack 1 hour. Refrigerate 8 hours. Cut into squares. Store in the refrigerator. Drizzle each serving with raspberry sauce and sprinkle with powdered sugar, as desired. Refrigerate leftovers.

Makes 16 servings.

MARY DOW'S HOMEMADE CUSTARD WITH BERRIES

Homemade custard . . . good with thawed frozen berries too.

1½ cups heavy whipping cream

**½ cup granulated sugar mixed in a small bowl
with 1 tablespoon cornstarch**

4 egg yolks
2 teaspoons pure vanilla extract

fresh raspberries
fresh strawberries

Cook whipping cream in a 2-quart saucepan over medium heat until cream just comes to a boil, about 6–8 minutes. Remove from heat.

Whisk sugar mixture and egg yolks with a wire whisk in a medium bowl until mixture is light and creamy, about 3–4 minutes.

Gradually whisk hot whipping cream into beaten egg yolk mixture. Return mixture to same saucepan. Stir in vanilla extract. Cook over medium heat, stirring constantly, until custard is thickened and coats back of a metal spoon, about 3–4 minutes (do not boil). Remove from heat; cool slightly before serving or cool and refrigerate.

Serve warm custard over berries in dessert dishes. Refrigerate leftovers.

Makes 6 servings.

NELAN'S LAYERED DESSERT

There's enough to share, but . . .

2 cream-filled sponge cakes such as Twinkies
2 scoops raspberry ice cream, slightly softened
chocolate ice cream topping
chopped pecans
thawed nondairy whipped topping
1 cherry

Cut the sponge cakes in half lengthwise. Place one cut cake in a small bowl. Add a scoop of raspberry ice cream. Drizzle with chocolate topping. Sprinkle with pecans.

Repeat with another layer starting with cake, ice cream, chocolate topping and pecans.

Top with thawed whipped topping. Top with a cherry. Serve.

Makes 1 serving.

SPICED PANNA COTTA WITH RASPBERRY ORANGE SAUCE

Panna cotta, Italian for cooked cream . . . a light and luscious dessert.

1 envelope unflavored gelatin
⅓ cup cold water
2 cups heavy cream
1 cup dairy sour cream
½ cup granulated sugar
½ teaspoon whole cloves
1 cinnamon stick
1 teaspoon pure vanilla extract

Sauce
2 cups frozen unsweetened
  raspberries
½ cup orange marmalade
¼ cup granulated sugar
¼ teaspoon ground cloves
¼ teaspoon ground nutmeg

Mix gelatin and water in a small bowl; let stand 15 minutes to soften.

Mix cream, sour cream, sugar, cloves and cinnamon stick in a medium saucepan. Stir gently over medium heat until mixture comes to a simmer. Remove from heat; strain mixture into a bowl; discard cloves and cinnamon stick. Whisk gelatin mixture into strained hot cream mixture until gelatin is completely dissolved. Stir in vanilla.

Lightly coat six ¾-cup ramekins with cooking spray. Spoon panna cotta equally into ramekins. Refrigerate and cool. Cover and chill until set, at least 4 hours or overnight.

Sauce: Thaw raspberries in a microwave-safe dish and crush using a fork. Stir in remaining sauce ingredients. Microwave 1 minute on high. Cool.

To serve, run a knife around each panna cotta and invert on a dessert plate. Top with sauce as desired. Refrigerate leftovers.

Makes 6 servings.

STUFFED POACHED PEARS WITH RASPBERRY SAUCE

Serve this elegant desert for that special dinner.

2 tablespoons part-skim ricotta cheese
2 tablespoons crumbled bleu cheese
2 tablespoons chopped pecans
1 tablespoon fresh lemon juice

2 fresh pears, peeled, halved and cored
⅛ teaspoon ground nutmeg

½ cup white wine or white grape juice

1 10-ounce package frozen red raspberries in syrup, thawed
2 teaspoons cornstarch

Mix ricotta cheese, bleu cheese, pecans and lemon juice in a small bowl. Fill center of pear with mixture. Sprinkle top with nutmeg.

Heat wine to a boil in medium skillet. Place pears, stuffing side up, in skillet. Cover. Reduce heat to medium-low and simmer 10 minutes or until pears are tender.

Mash and strain raspberries; discard seeds. Measure ¾ cup raspberry juice, adding water if needed.

Whisk cornstarch into raspberry juice; pour into a small saucepan. Heat and stir mixture until sauce is thickened slightly and just begins to bubble.

To serve, place 3 tablespoons sauce on a dessert plate and top with a pear half. Refrigerate leftovers.

Makes 4 servings.

RASPBERRIES ROMANOFF

Simple and delicious.

1 pint fresh raspberries
2 tablespoons granulated sugar
2 tablespoons orange flavored liqueur or ½ teaspoon
   freshly grated orange peel

⅓ cup frozen nondairy whipped topping, thawed
½ teaspoon pure vanilla extract
½ pint vanilla ice cream, softened

Mix raspberries, sugar and liqueur in a large glass bowl. Cover and refrigerate at least 2 hours, stirring occasionally.

Mix whipped topping, vanilla extract and ice cream in a bowl. Fold mixture into raspberry mixture. Spoon into dessert glasses. Garnish with additional fresh raspberries and serve immediately. Refrigerate leftovers.

Makes 5 servings.

RASPBERRY CHEESECAKE PARFAITS

A quick and delicious dessert to serve to family or unexpected guests.

1¼ cups coarsely crushed graham cracker crumbs
3 tablespoons melted butter, cooled
2 tablespoons granulated sugar

1 8-ounce package cream cheese, softened
1 14-ounce can sweetened condensed milk
1 small lemon, juiced
1 teaspoon pure vanilla extract

1 12-ounce package frozen unsweetened red raspberries,
   slightly thawed

Mix coarse crumbs, butter and sugar in a medium bowl; set aside.

Beat cream cheese in a mixing bowl on medium speed until fluffy. Add sweetened condensed milk, lemon juice and vanilla. Beat until creamy.

Layer equal amount of graham cracker crumbs, cream cheese mixture and raspberries in dessert glasses. Serve immediately or refrigerate. Refrigerate leftovers.

Makes 6 servings.

Variation: Fresh raspberries.

RASPBERRY FOOL

So simple . . . elegant and delicious!

3 cups fresh raspberries, rinsed, divided

1 cup heavy whipping cream
¼ cup granulated sugar
½ teaspoon pure vanilla extract

Process 1½ cups raspberries in a food processor until pureed. Press puree through a sieve; discard seeds.

Beat whipping cream, sugar and vanilla in mixing bowl to soft peaks. Gently fold in raspberry puree.

Spoon into dessert glasses. Top with remaining raspberries. Cover and refrigerate. Chill at least an hour before serving. Refrigerate leftovers.

Makes 4 servings.

RASPBERRY TIRAMISU

A delicious make ahead dessert.

¾ cup seedless raspberry jam
½ teaspoon freshly grated orange zest
5 tablespoons fresh orange juice

1 cup whipping cream
¼ cup granulated sugar
1 teaspoon pure vanilla extract

1 pound mascarpone cheese,
   room temperature
2 tablespoons orange liqueur or
   fresh orange juice

28 soft ladyfingers
3½ cups fresh raspberries

powdered sugar

Mix jam, orange zest and 5 tablespoons orange juice in a bowl; set aside.

Mix mascarpone cheese and 2 tablespoons orange liqueur or fresh orange juice
in a large bowl.

Beat whipping cream, ¼ cup granulated sugar and vanilla in another bowl to soft
peaks; stir one-quarter of mixture into mascarpone mixture to combine. Fold in
remaining whipped cream into mascarpone cheese mixture.

Line bottom of 13x9x2-inch glass baking dish with half of ladyfingers. Spread half
the jam mixture over ladyfingers. Spread half the mascarpone mixture over jam.
Cover with half the raspberries.

Repeat layering with remaining ladyfingers, jam mixture, mascarpone mixture and
raspberries. Cover and refrigerate until well chilled. Dust with powdered sugar
when serving. Store in the refrigerator.

Makes 10 servings.

Variation: Use pound cake cut into 3x1x1½-inch pieces in place of ladyfingers.

VANILLA CRÈME BRÛLÉE WITH RASPBERRIES

Fresh raspberries are used in this classic custard.

6 tablespoons red raspberry jam
1 pint fresh raspberries, divided, rinsed and dried

6 egg yolks
6 tablespoons granulated sugar
1 vanilla bean, split lengthwise
1½ cups whipping cream
¼ cup golden brown sugar, packed, divided

Preheat oven to 325°.

Spread 1 tablespoon jam onto bottom of each of six ¾-cup custard cups. Place 6 raspberries, sideways, into jam in each cup; press gently.

Whisk yolks and granulated sugar in a medium bowl until blended. Scrape in seeds from split vanilla bean. Gradually whisk in whipping cream.

Divide mixture among the custard cups; place in a 13x9x2-inch baking pan. Place baking pan in oven. Pour enough hot water into the baking pan to come halfway up sides of custard cups.

Bake custard until center is set, about 40 minutes. Remove baking pan from oven. Let custard cups cool in water 30 minutes. Remove custard cups from water; chill 8 hours.

Preheat broiler.

Sprinkle 2 teaspoons brown sugar on top of each custard. Place on a baking sheet. Broil until sugar just starts to caramelize, turning sheet for even browning, about 2 minutes. Chill until top hardens, about 2 hours.

Serve garnished with fresh raspberries. Refrigerate leftovers. Makes 6 servings.

ZABAGLIONE

A special dessert that is simple to prepare. Serve with thin sweet wafers.

½ cup sweet Marsala wine or white grape juice
2 tablespoons granulated sugar
¼ teaspoon pure vanilla extract
4 egg yolks
pinch of salt

3 cups fresh raspberries
grated chocolate

Mix wine, sugar and vanilla in the top of a double boiler over hot water (not boiling water). Cook and stir until sugar dissolves.

Add egg yolks and salt. Cook mixture, beating with an electric mixer about 7–9 minutes or until mixture thickens, mounds and almost triples in volume.

Serve warm over raspberries. Sprinkle with grated chocolate as desired. Refrigerate leftovers.

Makes 6 servings.

Frozen
Desserts

CHOCOLATE ICE CREAM WITH RASPBERRY ALMOND SAUCE

Invite your neighbor for a dish of this luscious ice cream.

Ice Cream
3 large egg yolks
¼ cup granulated sugar

1½ cups heavy cream
½ cup whole milk
4 ounces 70% cacao extra bittersweet chocolate baking bar
½ teaspoon pure vanilla extract

Sauce
1 10-ounce package frozen raspberries in syrup, thawed
1 teaspoon fresh lemon juice
¼ teaspoon almond extract
½ teaspoon unflavored gelatin

Ice Cream: Whisk egg yolks and sugar in a medium bowl; set aside.

Heat cream, milk and chocolate in a medium saucepan over medium heat, whisking often, until chocolate melts and mixture is hot but not boiling. Pour hot mixture into the egg yolk mixture, whisking constantly, then return the mixture to the pan. Heat over low heat to 170°, or until mixture coats a spoon, stirring constantly. Immediately strain into a bowl and whisk in the vanilla. Cool mixture in the refrigerator, whisking often.

Freeze in an ice cream freezer following manufacturer's directions until ice cream has the consistency of whipped cream. Transfer to a plastic food container and store in the freezer. Best if eaten the same day it is made. If frozen, let soften in the refrigerator 20 minutes before serving. Freeze leftovers.

Sauce: Press raspberries through a fine sieve into a small saucepan; discard seeds. Add lemon juice, almond extract and gelatin to pan. Let rest 5 minutes or until gelatin is softened. Cook over medium heat, stirring constantly, until gelatin is dissolved and mixture is hot. Remove from heat; cool slightly. Serve as desired over ice cream. Refrigerate leftovers.

Makes 1 quart.

FROSTY RASPBERRY
MACADAMIA DESSERT

A delicious do ahead dessert to prepare for special company.

1 cup crushed vanilla wafers
½ cup finely chopped macadamia nuts
¼ cup butter, melted

1 14-ounce can sweetened condensed milk
3 tablespoons fresh orange juice
3 tablespoons fresh lemon juice
½ teaspoon pure vanilla extract

1 10-ounce package frozen sweetened raspberries, thawed
1 8-ounce container frozen nondairy whipped topping, thawed
fresh raspberries
additional whipped topping

Preheat oven to 375°.
Butter a 9-inch springform pan.

Mix vanilla wafer crumbs, nuts and butter in a bowl until well blended. Press mixture onto the bottom of prepared baking pan. Bake 8 minutes. Cool completely in pan on a wire rack.

Beat sweetened condensed milk, orange juice, lemon juice and vanilla extract in a large bowl on low speed until blended. Stir in raspberries. Fold in thawed whipped topping. Spoon mixture onto prepared crust. Cover and freeze until firm, about 3 hours.

Let stand at room temperature 15 minutes before serving. Garnish each serving with raspberries and whipped topping. Freeze leftovers.

Makes 12 servings.

JANE'S ICE CREAM SANDWICHES

Cousin Jane lives in Texas and enjoys ice cream sandwiches, purchased or homemade!

1 cup vanilla ice cream
1 cup raspberry ice cream
1 cup finely chopped roasted almonds, divided
30 chocolate chip cookies, purchased or homemade

raspberry jam

Stir both ice creams together in a bowl until slightly softened. Stir in ½ cup almonds. Freeze about 30 minutes or until firm enough to hold its shape.

Thinly spread 15 cookies on one side with raspberry jam. Spoon about 2 tablespoons of ice cream mixture on one side of remaining 15 cookies. Top with the 15 jam-covered cookies, jam-side on ice cream; press together.

Roll edges in remaining almonds. Freeze 1–2 hours or until firm. Wrap sandwiches individually in plastic wrap and place in a plastic freezer bag. Store up to 2 weeks.

Makes 15 sandwiches.

MASCARPONE RASPBERRY ICE CREAM

Serve a bowl of this tasty dessert to ice cream lovers.

2 cups half-and-half
1 cup granulated sugar

1 8-ounce container mascarpone cheese
1½ teaspoons pure vanilla extract
1 teaspoon finely grated fresh lemon zest

1½ cups fresh or frozen raspberries

Heat half-and-half and sugar in a medium saucepan over medium-low heat, stirring until sugar is dissolved. Remove from heat and let cool.

Whisk in mascarpone cheese and vanilla. Stir in lemon zest. Let cool, then refrigerate briefly. (Do not let buttery yellow layer on top solidify.) Pour mixture into the container of an ice cream maker. Freeze according to manufacturer's directions.

When mixture is frozen, add raspberries and let ice cream maker run for a few minutes more. Remove paddle; cover and freeze until ready to serve. Freeze leftovers.

Makes 8 servings.

PEACH AND RASPBERRY ICE CREAM

An ice cream that is simple to prepare . . . and delicious.

3 medium fresh peaches, peeled, pits removed, mashed in a bowl
1 cup fresh or thawed frozen red raspberries, pureed
2 cups whipping cream or half-and-half
1 14-ounce can sweetened condensed milk
2½ teaspoons pure vanilla extract
½ teaspoon pure almond extract

Place all ingredients in an ice cream maker; mix well. Freeze according to manufacturer's directions. Freeze leftovers.

Makes 1½ quarts.

BERRY GRANITA

Raspberries and strawberries are found in this Italian ice . . . simple to make and always a refreshing treat.

1 cup freshly squeezed orange juice
¾ cup cold water
½ cup honey
¼ cup granulated sugar
2 teaspoons orange zest
3½ cups fresh strawberries, hulled and quartered
2 6-ounce packages fresh raspberries

Mix orange juice, water, honey, sugar, orange zest and half the berries in a blender. Pulse, and then puree until almost smooth. Add remaining berries and puree until smooth. Test for sweetness; add more honey, if needed.

Pour mixture into a 13x9x2-inch nonstick metal baking pan. Freeze until edges become icy and center is slushy, about 1 hour. Stir the icy edges into middle of pan with a fork, repeating this step every 30 minutes until granita is solid, about 3 hours.

When solid, scrape granita down the length of pan with a fork, forming flaky ice crystals. Cover tightly and freeze. Scrape granita into bowls. Serve immediately. Freeze leftovers.

Makes 6 servings.

RASPBERRY SORBET

This dessert is simple to make and so refreshing.

¾ **cup granulated sugar**
¼ **cup lime juice**
¼ **cup light corn syrup**
¼ **cup cold water**

4 cups fresh or frozen raspberries
¼ **teaspoon salt**

Mix sugar, lime juice, corn syrup and water in a saucepan over medium heat. Cook and stir until sugar dissolves and mixture is clear. Remove from heat; cool 5 minutes. Pour mixture into a blender.

Add raspberries and salt. Process until smooth. Strain mixture through a fine-mesh sieve into a large container; discard seeds. Cover strained mixture and refrigerate at least 2 hours.

Pour mixture into the canister of an ice cream maker. Freeze according to manufacturer's instructions. Remove from canister. Freeze leftovers.

Makes 6 servings.

Pastries
Tortes
Tarts

CHOCOLATE MOUSSE NAPOLEONS WITH RASPBERRIES

Puff pastry is used for these delicious pastries.

1 sheet puff pastry (half of a 17-ounce package)

1 cup whipping cream
powdered sugar, divided
½ teaspoon pure vanilla extract
⅔ cup semi-sweet chocolate chips, melted, cooled, divided
1¼ cups fresh raspberries, rinsed and patted dry

Thaw pastry sheet at room temperature 40 minutes.
Preheat oven to 400°.

Unfold pastry on a lightly floured surface. Cut into 3 strips along fold marks. Cut each strip into 4 rectangles. Place 1 inch apart on baking sheet. Bake 12 minutes or until golden. Remove from baking sheet and cool completely on a wire rack.

Beat whipping cream, 1 tablespoon powdered sugar and vanilla in a mixing bowl on high speed until soft peaks form. Spoon half the whipped cream mixture into another bowl; fold one-third melted chocolate into one bowl.

Split baked pastries into two layers, making 24 layers.

Spread 8 pastry layers equally with chocolate cream mixture, then top with 8 pastry layers.

Top equally with remaining whipped cream, raspberries and remaining pastry layers. Sprinkle with powdered sugar. Drizzle equally with remaining melted chocolate.

Serve immediately or refrigerate up to 4 hours. Refrigerate leftovers.

Makes 8 servings.

EASY RASPBERRY CHEESE DANISH

Cut and serve this easy to prepare Danish for a special treat.

2 10-ounce cans refrigerated crescent roll dough

2 8-ounce packages cream cheese, cut into small pieces
½ cup granulated sugar
½ cup raspberry jam
2 teaspoons fresh lemon juice
1 teaspoon pure vanilla extract
2 teaspoons sour cream or heavy cream

Glaze
1 cup powdered sugar
1 tablespoon butter, softened
1 tablespoon fresh orange juice or as needed

Preheat oven to 350°.
Grease a 13x9-inch baking pan.

Line bottom of prepared baking pan with 1 can crescent roll dough. Pinch all seams to seal.

Mix cream cheese, granulated sugar, jam, lemon juice, vanilla and sour cream in a large bowl. Spread mixture on top of dough. Layer remaining can of crescent dough roll on top of filling.

Bake 20–35 minutes. Remove from oven; cool in pan.

Mix powdered sugar, butter and enough orange juice in a bowl to a drizzle consistency. Drizzle over cooled Danish. Refrigerate leftovers.

Makes 10 servings.

JAM DOUGHNUTS

Surprise the gang with homemade raspberry jam doughnuts.

¾ cup whole milk
¼ cup butter or margarine
¼ cup granulated sugar
½ teaspoon salt

½ teaspoon pure vanilla extract
1 teaspoon freshly grated lemon zest

1 package dry yeast, dissolved
  in ¼ cup warm water (not hot)
2 eggs, divided
3½ to 4 cups all-purpose flour
⅔ cup raspberry jam
corn oil for deep frying

Stir milk, butter, sugar and salt in a saucepan over medium heat until butter is melted. Pour mixture into a large mixing bowl; stir in vanilla and lemon zest. Cool mixture until barely warm to touch, and then stir in the dissolved yeast (do not put yeast in hot mixture).

Separate one egg; reserve the white for later. Beat the yolk and 1 whole egg in a small bowl; add to milk mixture. Add 3 cups flour; beat with a wooden spoon until moist dough is formed. Knead dough on a lightly floured surface, adding enough remaining flour to create dough that is soft but not sticky. Place in a greased bowl; cover with clean kitchen towel and let set until double in bulk. Punch dough down and roll out on a floured surface to a ¼-inch thickness.

Cut dough with a 3-inch biscuit cutter. Spoon a dollop of jam onto the center of half the rounds. Beat the egg white in a small bowl, then lightly brush it on the dough surrounding the jam. Top with the remaining dough rounds and press to seal. Place on a baking sheet; cover with a clean kitchen towel and let rest 10 minutes.

Heat corn oil in a deep fryer to 370°.

Place doughnut in hot oil using a perforated metal spatula. Fry only a few dough-nuts at a time about 3–4 minutes or until golden brown on both sides; do not crowd. Drain on paper towels. Repeat.

Makes 2 dozen.

PEAR AND BERRY STRUDEL WITH CARAMEL RASPBERRY SAUCE

Dried raspberries and dried cranberries are used in this strudel.

1 sheet puff pastry
(half of a 17-ounce package),
thawed

¼ cup dried raspberries
¼ cup dried cranberries

½ cup brown sugar, packed
2 tablespoons cornstarch
½ teaspoon ground cinnamon

2 large Bosc pears, peeled,
cored and diced
1 teaspoon pure vanilla extract
1 egg beaten in a cup with
1 tablespoon cold water

Sauce
¾ cup purchased caramel topping,
heated and mixed in a small bowl
with ¼ cup seedless raspberry jam

Preheat oven to 375°.
Line a baking sheet with cooking parchment paper or lightly grease.

Place dried raspberries and dried cranberries in a bowl and cover with boiling water; let stand 5 minutes, then drain.

Mix sugar, cornstarch and cinnamon in medium bowl, add pears, drained berries and vanilla extract; stir until coated.

Unroll thawed pastry sheet on a lightly floured surface. Roll out into a 14x11-inch rectangle. With the long side facing you, spoon the pear mixture onto the lower third of pastry to within an inch of each end. Starting at the long side, roll up like a jelly roll. Tuck ends under to seal. Place seam side down on prepared baking sheet. Brush with the egg mixture. Cut several 2-inch long slits on top, 2 inches apart. Bake about 25 minutes or until golden. Cool in the baking sheet on a wire rack 15 minutes. Remove from baking sheet. Heat topping according to instructions on packaging. Mix topping with jam. Cut strudel and serve with warm sauce. Refrigerate leftovers.

Makes 6 servings.

PEAR RASPBERRY PUFF PASTRY

Bake the pastry shells ahead of time. Then whip the cream just before serving and top with berries for a delicious dessert.

4 puff pastry shells thawed and baked following package directions; cool

½ cup heavy cream
½ teaspoon pure vanilla extract
⅓ cup powdered sugar
2 cups fresh raspberries, rinsed and patted dry
2 fresh pears, peeled and thinly sliced

Beat cream, vanilla and powdered sugar in a mixing bowl to soft peaks. Spoon whipped cream evenly into cooled pastry shells. Top equally with raspberries and pears. Serve. Refrigerate leftovers.

Makes 4 servings.

RASPBERRY CREAM CHEESE PASTRY

The perfect treat for that afternoon coffee or midnight snack.

Filling
**1 3-ounce package cream cheese,
  softened
1 egg yolk
2 tablespoons granulated sugar
1 teaspoon all-purpose flour
1 teaspoon pure vanilla extract
¼ cup raspberry preserves**

Dough
**2½ cups all-purpose flour
⅔ cup butter**

**½ cup dairy sour cream
4 to 6 tablespoons cold water**

Topping
**2 tablespoons butter, melted
2 tablespoons granulated sugar**

Glaze
**½ cup powdered sugar mixed in
  a small bowl with 1 tablespoon
  orange juice and ½ teaspoon pure
  vanilla extract until smooth**

Filling: Mix all filling ingredients except raspberry preserves in a medium bowl until smooth; set aside.

Dough: Process flour and butter with a pastry blender until coarse crumbs form. Stir in sour cream. Add 1 tablespoon water at a time, and mix with a fork just until flour mixture is moistened. Divide dough in half. Shape into 2 balls then flatten. Cover and refrigerate 30 minutes. Roll out half of dough on a lightly floured surface into a 12x8-inch rectangle. Cut into six 4-inch squares. Place 2 teaspoons filling and 1 teaspoon raspberry preserves in center of each square. Fold one corner of dough over filling to form a triangle. Seal edges with a fork. Repeat with remaining dough and filling. Place on lightly greased baking sheets.

Preheat oven to 400°.

Topping: Brush tops with 2 tablespoons melted butter and sprinkle with 2 tablespoons granulated sugar. Bake 20–25 minutes. Remove from oven. Cool slightly. Drizzle with glaze. Serve warm. Refrigerate leftovers.

Makes 12 servings.

BROWNIE FRESH BERRY TORTE

Blackberries and raspberries top this brownie torte.

½ cup all-purpose flour
¼ teaspoon baking soda
¼ teaspoon salt
1 cup semi-sweet chocolate chips

½ cup butter or margarine
1 cup granulated sugar
2 eggs
1 teaspoon pure vanilla extract
⅓ cup dark cocoa powder

Topping
½ cup whipping cream, whipped with ¼ cup granulated sugar
   and ½ teaspoon pure vanilla extract
¾ cup each: fresh blackberries and raspberries, rinsed
   and patted dry

Preheat oven to 350°.
Wax paper line and grease a 9-inch round cake pan.

Mix flour, baking soda, salt and chocolate chips in a bowl; set aside.

Melt butter in a medium saucepan over low heat. Remove from heat. Stir in
1 cup sugar, eggs and 1 teaspoon vanilla. Stir in cocoa until blended. Stir in flour
mixture. Spread batter into prepared baking pan.

Bake 20–25 minutes or until a wooden pick inserted in center comes out slightly
sticky. Cool in pan on a wire rack 15 minutes. Invert onto wire rack; remove wax
paper. Turn torte right side up and cool completely.

Spread top with whipped cream. Top with berries. Store in the refrigerator.

Makes 8 servings.

CHOCOLATE TORTE WITH RASPBERRY SAUCE

An elegant dessert!

Torte
8 1-ounce squares semi-sweet baking chocolate
½ cup butter
½ cup powdered sugar
4 eggs
½ cup finely ground almonds
½ cup dairy sour cream
¼ cup all-purpose flour

Frosting
4 1-ounce squares semi-sweet baking chocolate, melted
2 tablespoons butter, melted
2 tablespoons honey

Sauce
1 10-ounce package frozen raspberries in syrup, thawed
2 teaspoons cornstarch

Preheat oven to 350°. Grease a round 9-inch cake pan. Line with aluminum cooking foil, letting excess go over the edges. Grease foil; set aside.

Torte: Melt 8 squares baking chocolate and ½ cup butter in a small saucepan over low heat, stirring constantly, until smooth; set aside. Beat powdered sugar and eggs in a large bowl on high speed until light and foamy, about 5 minutes. Add ground almonds, sour cream and flour; beat until well mixed. Add chocolate mixture; beat until well mixed. Spread batter into prepared pan. Bake about 30–35 minutes or until firm to touch. Do not overbake. Cool on a wire rack 30 minutes. Remove from pan by lifting on foil. Remove foil; place torte on a serving plate.

Frosting: Place all frosting ingredients in a small saucepan. Cook and stir over low heat until melted and smooth. Frost top and sides of torte. Refrigerate until firm, about 1 hour.

Sauce: Press raspberries through a fine wire strainer; discard seeds. Place strained raspberries and cornstarch in a small saucepan. Stir and cook over medium heat until mixture comes to a full boil; boil, stirring constantly, until slightly thickened. Cool slightly, then stir. Cover and refrigerate. To serve, spoon a small portion of sauce on each individual dessert plate. Top with a slice of torte and serve. Refrigerate leftovers. Makes 12 servings.

FLOURLESS CHOCOLATE TORTE WITH RASPBERRY SAUCE

Mocha whipped cream and raspberry sauce tops this sweet torte.

Torte
1¼ cups butter
¾ cup unsweetened cocoa powder
2 cups granulated sugar, divided
6 eggs, separated
¼ cup cold water
1 teaspoon pure vanilla extract
1 cup blanched, sliced almonds,
toasted and ground
½ cup plain dry bread crumbs

Raspberry Sauce
1 12-ounce bag unsweetened
frozen raspberries, thawed
3 tablespoons fresh orange juice
½ cup granulated sugar

Mocha Cream
1 cup whipping cream
2 tablespoons powdered sugar
1½ teaspoons powdered instant
coffee dissolved in 1 teaspoon
cold water
½ teaspoon pure vanilla extract

Preheat oven to 350°. Grease and flour a 9-inch springform pan.

Torte: Melt butter in a saucepan over low heat. Stir in cocoa and 1½ cups sugar until smooth; cool to room temperature. Beat egg yolks in a large bowl until thick. Gradually beat in chocolate mixture; stir in water and vanilla. Stir in almonds and bread crumbs. Beat egg whites in another bowl until foamy. Gradually beat in remaining ½ cup sugar to soft peaks. Fold one-third mixture into chocolate mixture. Fold chocolate mixture into remaining egg whites. Pour into prepared pan. Bake 50–60 minutes or until a wooden pick comes out clean. Cool 10 minutes; remove pan. Cool completely. Slice. Store in the refrigerator.

Raspberry Sauce: Push raspberries through strainer to remove seeds. Discard seeds. Cook strained raspberries, orange juice and sugar over medium heat until sauce is thick and syrupy. Chill.

Mocha Cream: Mix whipping cream, powdered sugar, instant coffee mixture and vanilla extract in a bowl; beat until stiff.

When serving, place a circle of sauce onto dessert plates. Add a wedge of torte and top with mocha cream. Refrigerate leftovers. Makes 10 servings.

NO-BAKE RASPBERRY TORTE

Slice and garnish this raspberry torte with fresh mint.

2 cups graham cracker crumbs
½ cup butter, melted
¼ cup granulated sugar

1 16-ounce package miniature marshmallows
1 cup whole milk

2 cups heavy whipping cream, whipped in a large bowl
with 2 tablespoons granulated sugar and 1 teaspoon
pure vanilla extract
4 cups fresh raspberries, rinsed and patted dry
½ cup finely chopped pecans or almonds

Mix graham cracker crumbs, butter and ¼ cup sugar in a bowl; reserve ¼ cup mixture. Press remaining mixture onto bottom and 1½ inches up sides of a 9-inch springform pan.

Cook and stir marshmallows with milk in a large saucepan over medium-low heat until marshmallows are melted and mixture is smooth. Remove from heat. Cool completely in saucepan.

Fold in whipped cream, raspberries and pecans. Pour mixture into prepared crust. Top with remaining crumb mixture. Cover and refrigerate 8 hours before serving. Remove sides of pan. Serve. Refrigerate leftovers.

Makes 12 servings.

ALMOND CRUSTED FRESH RASPBERRY TART

Serve plain or topped with sweetened whipped cream.

Crust
1½ cups all-purpose flour
½ cup granulated sugar
½ cup cold butter, cut into pieces
1 egg
½ teaspoon pure vanilla extract
½ teaspoon pure almond extract
½ cup finely chopped almonds
1 egg white, slightly beaten

Filling
3 cups fresh raspberries, washed and patted dry
2 tablespoons granulated sugar

Preheat oven to 400°.

Crust: With mixer on medium speed, beat flour, ½ cup granulated sugar, butter, egg and extracts in a large bowl until coarse crumbs form.

Stir in almonds by hand. Press mixture onto bottom and 1 inch up sides of a 10-inch springform pan. Chill 1 hour. Brush with egg white. Bake 15 minutes. Remove from oven.

Filling: Place raspberries on partially baked crust. Return to oven and continue baking until crust is golden brown, about 10 minutes. Sprinkle with 2 tablespoons sugar. Serve warm. Refrigerate leftovers.

Makes 8 servings.

CHOCOLATE RASPBERRY TARTLETS

Chocolate raspberry individual tartlets . . . delicious.

12 tablespoons butter
6 tablespoons granulated sugar
6 tablespoons unsweetened
  cocoa powder
1½ cups cake flour

1 cup heavy cream
14 ounces semi-sweet
  chocolate chips
3 cups fresh raspberries
powdered sugar

Process butter and sugar in food processor until creamy. Add cocoa; process until smooth. Add flour and pulse until crumbly.

Divide dough into six equal pieces. Flatten each piece into a disk and wrap in plastic wrap. Refrigerate 30 minutes. Remove 1 piece of dough at a time and roll out into a 6-inch circle between 2 pieces of plastic wrap. Remove the top piece of plastic wrap and invert dough over a 4½-inch nonstick tartlet pan with removable bottom. Leave plastic wrap on top side and press dough into bottom and sides of pan. Trim excess dough and carefully remove plastic wrap. Repeat with remaining dough. Refrigerate tartlet shells 30 minutes.

Preheat oven to 375°.

Prick bottom of tartlet shells all over with a fork. Bake about 15 minutes or until dough looks dry. Remove from oven; cool completely in pans.

Bring heavy cream to a simmer in a saucepan over medium heat. Remove from heat; add chocolate. Let stand until chocolate melts, then whisk gently to combine. Cool to room temperature.

Pour ⅓ cup chocolate mixture into each tartlet shell. Refrigerate until filling is firm, about 1 hour. Remove tartlets from pans to dessert plates. Arrange raspberries on top of filling. Sprinkle with powdered sugar as desired. Refrigerate leftovers.

Makes 6 servings.

PEACH AND RASPBERRY TART

Cream cheese, peaches and raspberries in an almond crust.

Crust
¼ **cup cold butter**
¼ **cup granulated sugar**
½ **cup sliced toasted almonds, chopped**
1¼ **cups all-purpose flour**
¼ **teaspoon baking soda**
⅛ **teaspoon salt**

Topping
2 **medium-ripe peaches,**
   pitted and sliced
1 **cup fresh raspberries**
½ **cup peach jam, melted**
¼ **cup sliced toasted almonds**

Filling
1 **8-ounce package cream cheese, softened**
3 **tablespoons honey**
½ **teaspoon pure vanilla extract**
¼ **teaspoon pure almond extract**

Preheat oven to 350°.

Crust: Mix butter and sugar in a medium bowl until well blended. Add almonds, flour, baking soda and salt. Stir with a fork until blended. Press mixture onto the bottom and sides of a 9-inch tart pan with a removable bottom. Bake 25 minutes. Remove from oven; cool on a wire rack.

Filling: Beat cream cheese, honey and extracts in a bowl until smooth. Spread mixture into prepared crust.

Topping: Arrange peaches and raspberries on top of filling. Brush lightly with melted jam. Sprinkle with almonds. Serve immediately or refrigerate.

Makes 8 servings.

RUSTIC FRESH
BLACKBERRY RASPBERRY TART

Hint: Press out dough with floured fingertips for easy handling.

Crust
½ cup toasted slivered almonds, crushed
¾ cup all-purpose flour
¼ cup granulated sugar
⅛ teaspoon salt
3 tablespoons butter, cut into small pieces
2 tablespoons ice cold water
½ teaspoon pure vanilla extract

Filling
4 ounces cream cheese, softened
1 tablespoon granulated sugar
½ cup fresh raspberries, mashed
½ teaspoon pure vanilla extract
2 cups fresh blackberries
1 cup fresh raspberries
¼ cup raspberry jam, melted

Preheat oven to 400°.
Line a baking sheet with aluminum cooking foil.

Crust: Mix almonds, flour, ¼ cup granulated sugar and salt in a medium bowl. Cut in butter with a pastry blender until coarse crumbs form. Sprinkle with water and vanilla extract; stir and gather dough into a ball. Place dough in center of prepared baking sheet. Press out into a 10-inch circle. Flute edges. Bake until light brown around edges, about 12 minutes. Cool. Remove foil from crust and place crust on a serving plate.

Filling: Beat cream cheese, 1 tablespoon sugar, mashed raspberries and ½ teaspoon vanilla extract in a medium bowl until fluffy. Spread mixture evenly on cooled crust. Top with fresh berries. Drizzle evenly with melted jam. Store in the refrigerator.

Makes 4 servings.

Pie

APPLE CRANBERRY RASPBERRY PIE

Serve plain or with vanilla ice cream . . . good cold too.

1 double crust, unbaked

3 cups cored, peeled and chopped
   Granny Smith apples (about 3
   medium)
2 cups coarsely chopped
   fresh cranberries
1 10-ounce package frozen dry
   pack raspberries, thawed

1½ cups granulated sugar
3 tablespoons quick-cooking
   tapioca
½ teaspoon ground cinnamon
¼ teaspoon salt
1 teaspoon pure vanilla extract

1 large egg
1 tablespoon water
additional granulated sugar

Preheat oven to 350°.
Place one unbaked crust into a 9-inch pie plate; set aside.

Filling: Mix apples, cranberries and raspberries in a large bowl. Mix sugar, tapioca,
cinnamon, salt and extract in a small bowl. Add to fruit mixture in large bowl and
toss until coated. Spoon filling into unbaked crust.

Top with second unbaked crust. Trim ½ inch beyond edge. Fold top crust under
bottom crust edge to seal. Crimp and flute edges. Cut slits in top crust to vent.

Beat egg with 1 tablespoon water in a small bowl; brush mixture on top of pie.
Sprinkle top lightly with additional granulated sugar. Cover edges with aluminum
foil to prevent browning too fast.

Bake 25 minutes. Remove foil. Bake 25–35 minutes or until filling in center is
bubbly and apples test done. Serve warm. Refrigerate leftovers.

Makes 8 servings.

BLACKBERRY RASPBERRY PIE

A delightful pie to serve on warm summer days.

1 9-inch pastry shell, baked

Filling
3 cups fresh blackberries, rinsed
1 cup fresh raspberries, rinsed
⅔ cup granulated sugar
½ teaspoon pure vanilla extract

¼ cup cold water plus enough reserved juice to measure ¾ cup
¼ cup cornstarch

Topping
1 cup whipping cream
2 tablespoons granulated sugar
⅓ cup dairy sour cream
½ teaspoon pure vanilla extract

Filling: Mix first four ingredients in a medium bowl; let stand at room temperature 20 minutes. Strain and reserve juice.

Stir water-juice mixture with cornstarch in a small bowl until smooth; place into a medium saucepan. Cook over medium heat, stirring constantly, until mixture boils. Remove from heat; cool slightly. Stir in berries to coat. Spoon mixture into baked crust. Refrigerate until set, about 4 hours. Refrigerate leftovers.

Topping: Beat whipping cream and granulated sugar to soft peaks in a medium bowl. Add sour cream and vanilla; beat to stiff peaks.

Top pie with whipped cream when serving. Refrigerate leftovers.

Makes 8 servings.

BLACK BOTTOM RASPBERRY CREAM PIE

Variation: Use a 6-serving size chocolate pudding mix for filling.

Crust
1¾ cups crushed chocolate
    wafer cookies
½ cup butter, melted
¼ cup granulated sugar

Filling
½ cup granulated sugar
¼ cup unsweetened cocoa powder
2 tablespoons cornstarch
2½ cups whole milk
2 large egg yolks
1 large egg

4 ounces semisweet chocolate,
    finely chopped
2 tablespoons butter
1 teaspoon pure vanilla extract

Topping
3 half-pint containers fresh
    raspberries, rinsed and patted dry
1 cup whipping cream
2 tablespoons powdered sugar
1 teaspoon pure vanilla extract

Preheat oven to 350°.
Butter a 9-inch glass pie pan.

Crust: Mix all crust ingredients in a bowl; press onto bottom and up sides of prepared pie plate. Bake about 6–8 minutes or until set; chill.

Filling: Mix sugar, cocoa powder and cornstarch in a medium saucepan. Stir in ¼ cup milk until cornstarch dissolves. Whisk in remaining milk, egg yolks and egg. Cook and stir over medium-high heat until pudding boils and thickens. Remove from heat. Whisk in chocolate, butter and vanilla until smooth. Pour pudding into prepared crust. Cover and chill.

Topping: Press most of the raspberries, pointed side up, on top of pudding. Beat cream, powdered sugar and vanilla to soft peaks; spread over raspberries. Top with remaining raspberries; chill. Store in the refrigerator.

Makes 8 servings.

CHOCOLATE PECAN PIE WITH RASPBERRY SAUCE

Hint: If using frozen crust, get a deep-dish style (4-cup volume) and do not thaw.

1 unbaked 9-inch deep-dish pie crust

Filling
¾ cup semi-sweet chocolate chunks
3 large eggs
1 cup light corn syrup
½ cup granulated sugar
¼ cup butter or margarine, melted
1 teaspoon pure vanilla extract
1 cup pecan halves, coarsely chopped

Raspberry Sauce
3 tablespoons pure maple syrup
2 tablespoons granulated sugar
1 16-ounce package frozen raspberries (do not thaw)

Preheat oven to 350°.

Place unbaked crust into a 9-inch deep-dish pie pan; place pie pan on a baking sheet and set aside.

Filling: Sprinkle chocolate evenly in crust. Whisk eggs, corn syrup, sugar, butter and vanilla extract in a medium bowl with a wire whisk until well blended. Stir in pecans. Pour mixture over chocolate.

Bake 50–55 minutes or until a knife inserted 2 inches from center comes out almost clean. Cover with cooking foil if browning too fast. Cool on a wire rack. Store in the refrigerator.

Raspberry Sauce: Cook syrup and sugar in a saucepan over medium heat, stirring constantly until sugar dissolves. Add raspberries; cook, stirring constantly, until thickened, about 8 minutes. Pour mixture through fine-mesh strainer. Press with back of a spoon to squeeze out sauce; discard solids. Serve sauce warm over pie. Refrigerate leftovers.

Makes 8 servings.

CHOCOLATE VANILLA CHEESECAKE PIE WITH RASPBERRY SAUCE

Chocolate and vanilla . . . and raspberries!

Crust
**2 cups crème-filled chocolate
sandwich cookie crumbs**
5 tablespoons butter, melted

Filling
**2 8-ounce packages cream cheese,
softened**
½ cup granulated sugar
¼ cup half-and-half
1 teaspoon pure vanilla extract
2 eggs
2 tablespoons unsweetened cocoa powder

Topping
**1 10-ounce package frozen
raspberries, thawed, pureed
and strained**
fresh raspberries, rinsed

Preheat oven to 350°.

Crust: Mix crumbs and butter; press into a 9-inch glass pie pan.

Filling: Beat cream cheese in a mixing bowl until fluffy. Add sugar, half-and-half and vanilla extract. Beat until blended. Beat in eggs one at a time until blended. Place 1 cup mixture in a small bowl. Stir in cocoa powder.

Spoon half of the chocolate batter into prepared crust. Cover with the plain batter. Top with spoonfuls of remaining chocolate batter. Cut through batters with a thin spatula for a marbled effect.

Bake 35–40 minutes or until center is set. Cool slightly, then refrigerate. Chill well before serving. Store pie and sauce in the refrigerator.

Top pie with raspberry puree when serving. Garnish with raspberries.

Makes 10 servings.

CREAMY RASPBERRY LEMON PIE

Fresh raspberries top this lemony cream cheese pie.

Crust
1¼ cups graham cracker crumbs
6 tablespoons butter, melted
¼ cup granulated sugar

Filling
¼ cup raspberry preserves
1 8-ounce package cream cheese, softened
1 3.4-ounce package instant lemon flavor pudding mix
1 cup cold whole milk
2 teaspoons grated lemon peel
1 teaspoon pure vanilla extract

2 cups thawed nondairy whipped topping, divided
1 cup fresh raspberries, rinsed

Preheat oven to 375°.

Crust: Mix all crust ingredients in a bowl. Press firmly onto bottom and up sides of an ungreased 9-inch pie pan. Bake 6 minutes; cool completely.

Filling: Spoon raspberry preserves onto bottom of prepared crust.

Beat cream cheese, dry pudding mix, milk, lemon peel, and vanilla extract in a large bowl with a wire whisk until very well blended.

Gently stir in 1 cup whipped topping. Pour mixture over preserves. Top with the remaining whipped topping, then top with fresh raspberries. Refrigerate until firm, about 4 hours. Store in the refrigerator.

Makes 8 servings.

FRESH RASPBERRY GELATIN PIE

Add a dollop of thawed whipped topping or sweetened whipped cream when serving.

Crust
1½ cups graham cracker crumbs
¼ cup granulated sugar
⅓ cup butter, melted

Filling
4 cups fresh raspberries, rinsed

¼ cup granulated sugar
1 tablespoon cornstarch
1 cup cold water

1 3-ounce package raspberry flavored gelatin mix
½ teaspoon pure vanilla extract

Preheat oven to 350°.

Crust: Mix all crust ingredients in a bowl; press mixture onto bottom and a little up sides of a 9-inch glass pie pan. Bake 6 minutes; cool.

Filling: Place raspberries in the cooled crust.

Mix sugar, cornstarch and water in a small saucepan until smooth. Bring mixture to a boil, stirring constantly until thickened, about 2 minutes.

Remove from heat; stir in dry gelatin until dissolved. Stir in vanilla extract. Cool slightly. Carefully pour mixture over raspberries. Refrigerate. Chill until set, about 3 hours. Refrigerate leftovers.

Makes 6 servings.

FRESH RASPBERRY PIE

Fresh raspberry pie is always a welcomed dessert.

1 9-inch pie shell, baked

Filling
1 cup granulated sugar
3 tablespoons cornstarch
¼ teaspoon salt
1 cup cold water
4 cups fresh raspberries, rinsed and divided
1 tablespoon butter
½ teaspoon pure vanilla extract

Topping
1 cup whipping cream
1 tablespoon powdered sugar
1 teaspoon pure vanilla extract

Filling: Mix sugar, cornstarch, salt and water in a 2-quart saucepan until smooth.
Stir in 2 cups raspberries. Bring mixture to a boil; cool 1 minute, stirring constantly.
Stir in butter and vanilla extract. Cool completely, about 30 minutes.

Stir in remaining 2 cups raspberries. Spoon filling into cooled baked shell.
Refrigerate; chill before serving.

Topping: Beat all topping ingredients in a medium bowl to stiff peaks. Garnish
each serving of pie with a dollop of whipped cream. Store pie and topping in
the refrigerator.

Makes 8 servings.

FROZEN RASPBERRY YOGURT PIE

Enjoy this frosty treat on those long summer days.

¼ **cup toasted coconut**

2 **cups vanilla yogurt, divided**
1 **8-ounce container frozen whipped topping, thawed**
1 **10-ounce package unsweetened frozen raspberries,**
   thawed and drained
1 **7-ounce jar marshmallow creme**

Sprinkle coconut onto bottom of a 9-inch glass pie pan; set aside.

Place 1 cup yogurt and thawed whipped topping in a bowl; mix until blended. Remove 1 cup of the blended mixture; cover and refrigerate for later use.

Spoon remaining blended mixture into the pie plate. Spread evenly onto bottom and up sides of pie pan. Freeze until firm, about 1 hour.

Beat raspberries and marshmallow creme in a medium mixing bowl on low speed until blended. Stir in remaining 1 cup yogurt, then stir in the reserved 1 cup blended mixture until well blended.

Spoon mixture into frozen shell. Return to freezer and freeze until firm, about 3 hours. Store in the freezer.

Makes 8 servings.

GLAZED FRESH RASPBERRY PIE

Serve this delicious pie with sweetened whipped cream.

Pastry Shell
1 cup all-purpose flour
½ teaspoon salt
6 tablespoons cold
**   vegetable shortening**
2 to 3 tablespoons ice cold water

Filling
6 cups fresh raspberries,
**   rinsed and patted dry, divided**
1 cup granulated sugar
3 tablespoons cornstarch
½ cup fresh orange juice
1 teaspoon fresh lemon juice
1 teaspoon pure vanilla extract

Preheat oven to 475°.

Pastry Shell: Mix flour and salt in a small bowl. Cut in shortening until particles are the size of small peas. Sprinkle water, 1 tablespoon at a time, mixing with a fork until all flour is moistened and dough cleans side of bowl. Form dough into a ball. Flatten ball on a lightly floured pastry cloth. Roll out dough (use a cloth-covered rolling pin) 2 inches larger than a 9-inch pie pan. Fold rolled out dough in half then half again and place in a 9-inch pie pan. Trim overhang 1 inch past rim of pan; unfold and roll dough edges under, even with pan. Flute edges. Prick bottom and sides with a fork. Bake 8–10 minutes. Cool on a wire rack.

Filling: Mash enough raspberries to measure 1 cup. Mix sugar and cornstarch in a saucepan. Stir in orange juice and mashed raspberries. Cook, stirring constantly, until mixture boils and thickens. Boil and stir 1 minute. Remove from heat.

Stir in lemon juice and vanilla. Pour half the glaze into cooled baked pie shell; spread over bottom and up sides, covering completely. Top with remaining raspberries. Pour remaining glaze over raspberries. Refrigerate at least 3 hours before serving. Refrigerate leftovers.

Makes 6 servings.

LEMONADE RASPBERRY PIE

This frosty pie is sure to become a summertime favorite.

1 14-ounce can sweetened condensed milk
1 6-ounce can frozen lemonade concentrate, partially thawed
3 tablespoons seedless raspberry preserves

1 8-ounce container frozen nondairy whipped topping, thawed

1 6-ounce ready-made graham cracker crust, or homemade

fresh raspberries, rinsed and patted dry (for garnish)

Whisk first three ingredients in a large bowl until smooth. Fold in whipped topping. Pour mixture into crust. Freeze until firm, about 4 hours. Garnish with fresh raspberries when serving. Freeze leftovers.

Makes 8 servings.

NO-BAKE RASPBERRY CHIFFON CREAM CHEESE PIE

A no-bake make ahead pie the whole family will enjoy.

Crust
1½ cups graham cracker crumbs
¼ cup ground toasted almonds
¼ cup granulated sugar
⅓ cup butter, melted

Filling
1 8-ounce package cream cheese, softened
1 tablespoon butter, softened
6 tablespoons powdered sugar
1 teaspoon pure vanilla extract
1 cup whipping cream, stiffly whipped
1½ cups fresh raspberries, rinsed and patted dry

1 envelope unflavored gelatin, softened in ⅓ cup cold water for 5 minutes
1 10-ounce package frozen raspberries in syrup, thawed, pureed and strained, seeds discarded
1 teaspoon fresh lemon juice
5 tablespoons granulated sugar

fresh raspberries, rinsed and patted dry (for garnish)

Crust: Mix all crust ingredients in a bowl; press mixture onto bottom and up sides of a 9-inch pie pan. Chill.

Filling: Beat cream cheese, butter, powdered sugar and vanilla in a mixing bowl until smooth and creamy. Fold in whipped cream. Pour mixture into prepared crust. Top with 1½ cups fresh raspberries. Chill.

Heat gelatin mixture in a small saucepan over medium heat until completely dissolved. Stir in remaining filling ingredients; refrigerate 35 minutes, then spoon chilled mixture over fresh raspberries. Refrigerate and chill until set. Store in the refrigerator.

When serving, garnish with sweetened whipped cream and fresh raspberries, as desired. Refrigerate leftovers.

Makes 8 servings.

Recipe adapted from my book *I Love Pies You Don't Bake*.

RASPBERRY CREAM CHEESE PIE

A purchased pastry shell will make short work of this pie!

1 9-inch pastry shell, baked

Filling
**1 8-ounce package cream cheese,
  softened**
¼ cup granulated sugar
1 tablespoon fresh lemon juice
½ teaspoon pure vanilla extract

Topping
4 tablespoons cornstarch
⅔ cup granulated sugar
¼ teaspoon salt
¾ cup cold water
⅓ cup fresh lemon juice

3 cups fresh raspberries
1 tablespoon butter
2 cups sweetened whipped cream

Filling: Beat cream cheese, ¼ cup sugar, lemon juice and vanilla in a mixing bowl on medium speed until smooth. Spread mixture in bottom of baked pastry shell; set aside.

Topping: Mix cornstarch, ⅔ cup sugar and salt in a medium saucepan. Stir in water and lemon juice until well blended.

Stir in raspberries; cook over medium heat, stirring frequently, until mixture thickens and becomes clear. Remove from heat. Stir in butter. Cool completely. Spread over cream cheese filling. Chill for at least 2 hours. Spread with whipped cream. Refrigerate leftovers.

Makes 8 servings.

SODA CRACKER RASPBERRY PIE

A delectable pie.

Crust
4 egg whites
¼ teaspoon cream of tartar
1 teaspoon pure vanilla extract
1 cup granulated sugar
16 saltine crackers, crushed
½ cup chopped pecans

Filling
1 cup whipping cream
⅓ cup granulated sugar
1 teaspoon pure vanilla extract
3 cups fresh or frozen raspberries

Preheat oven to 325°.
Grease and flour a 9-inch glass pie pan.

Crust: Beat egg whites and cream of tartar in a large bowl until foamy. Beat in 1 teaspoon vanilla. Gradually beat in 1 cup sugar until stiff peaks form. Fold in crushed crackers and pecans.

Spoon mixture into prepared pie plate; spread over bottom and sides. Bake 35–40 minutes or until golden. Cool completely.

Filling: Beat cream, ⅓ cup sugar and 1 teaspoon vanilla extract in a large bowl to soft peaks. Gently fold in raspberries; spoon mixture into cooled baked crust. Store in the refrigerator.

Makes 8 servings.

STRAWBERRY RASPBERRY
MERINGUE PIE

Fresh berries over creamy filling in a meringue crust.

Meringue
2 egg whites
¼ teaspoon cream of tartar
½ cup granulated sugar

Filling
1 cup dairy sour cream
¾ cup powdered sugar
4 ounces cream cheese, softened
1 teaspoon freshly grated orange peel
1 tablespoon fresh orange juice
½ teaspoon pure vanilla extract

Topping
2 cups fresh strawberries, hulled
1 cup fresh raspberries, rinsed
   and patted dry
¼ cup apple jelly, melted

Preheat oven to 275°.
Grease bottom only of 9-inch pie pan.

Meringue: Beat egg whites and cream of tartar in a small mixing bowl on high speed until foamy. Gradually beat in ½ cup sugar until glossy and stiff peaks form, about 4 minutes. Spoon meringue over bottom and up sides of prepared pan. Bake 1 hour. Turn off oven. Leave meringue in oven with door closed for 45 minutes. Remove from oven; cool.

Filling: Beat all filling ingredients in a medium bowl on medium speed until creamy. Spoon mixture into cooled meringue shell; spread evenly over bottom and up sides of shell. Immediately refrigerate and chill until firm, about 2 hours.

Topping: Just before serving, arrange strawberries stem-side down on filling. Add raspberries all over. Drizzle melted jelly over berries. Cut and serve. Refrigerate leftovers.

Makes 8 servings.

WHITE CHOCOLATE MOUSSE PIE
WITH RASPBERRY SAUCE

White chocolate and raspberries . . . a special dessert.

Crust
1 9-inch pastry shell, baked

Filling
1 6-ounce package premium white chocolate baking squares
1 14-ounce can sweetened condensed milk
1 teaspoon pure vanilla extract

2 cups whipping cream, stiffly whipped

Sauce
3 cups fresh raspberries, rinsed, divided
¼ cup granulated sugar
½ teaspoon fresh lemon juice

Filling: Melt white chocolate with sweetened condensed milk in a saucepan over low heat. Stir in extract; spoon into a large bowl. Cool mixture to room temperature.

Gently fold in whipped cream. Spoon into cooled baked crust. Refrigerate. Chill until set, about 4 hours. Refrigerate leftovers.

Sauce: Process 2 cups raspberries and sugar in a food processor until pureed. Press through a fine sieve over a small bowl; discard solids. Add remaining 1 cup raspberries and lemon juice; stir. Cover and chill slightly before serving. Store in the refrigerator.

Top each serving with raspberry sauce when serving.

Makes 8 servings.

Preserves
Jam
Jelly
Marmalade

RASPBERRY PRESERVES

Try making these preserves when raspberries are plentiful.
Unsweetened frozen raspberries may be used, thawed, juice included.

4 cups red raspberries (1 pound, 6 ounces)
3½ cups granulated sugar
⅓ cup strained fresh lemon juice

1 teaspoon butter

Wash jars in hot soapy water, then rinse with hot water; drain well.
Prepare lids as manufacturer directs.

Rinse and sort raspberries; drain well. Stir raspberries, sugar and lemon juice in a large bowl using a rubber spatula. Let stand, stirring several times, until sugar has dissolved, about 2 hours.

Place mixture into a large skillet or saucepan. Add butter. Bring to a boil, stirring constantly, and boil rapidly for 6 minutes. Remove from heat. Skim off foam.

Ladle hot preserves immediately into prepared jars, leaving ¼-inch headspace. Wipe jar rim with a clean, damp cloth. Attach lid. Process filled jars in a boiling water canner for 10 minutes.

After jars cool, check seals by pressing the middle of each lid with your finger. If a lid springs back, it is not sealed and refrigeration is necessary.

Makes 3 half pints.

THREE BERRY FREEZER JAM

Spread this delicious jam on toast, muffins or scones, or use as a topping
for ice cream.

2 6-ounce containers fresh raspberries
2 6-ounce containers fresh blueberries
1 16-ounce container fresh strawberries, hulled and quartered
1 cup granulated sugar
½ cup fresh orange juice
2 tablespoons fresh lemon juice

Rinse berries and place in a large heavy saucepan. Add sugar and juices.

Bring to a boil, then reduce heat slightly and simmer uncovered 1½ hours or until
mixture is very thick and coats a spoon (when mixture starts to thicken, reduce
heat to low and stir often to avoid scorching).

Let cool, then spoon into sterilized freezer containers, filling each within ¼-inch of
tops. Cover tightly and freeze up to 1 year.

Makes 3 cups.

RASPBERRY JELLY

Tip: Use a jelly bag instead of cheesecloth.

4 cups prepared juice (you will need 5 pints ripe red raspberries)
1 box fruit pectin
1 teaspoon butter or margarine
5¼ cups granulated sugar, measured into a separate bowl

Fill a boiling water canner half full with water; bring to a simmer.

Wash jars and bands in hot soapy water, then rinse with hot water. Drain. Pour boiling water over flat lids in a saucepan. Let stand until ready to use.

Crush raspberries thoroughly. Place three layers of damp cheesecloth in a large bowl. Pour prepared fruit into cheesecloth. Tie closed, hang and let drip into bowl until dripping stops; gently squeeze bag to extract any remaining juice. Measure exactly 4 cups juice into an 8-quart saucepan.

Stir pectin into juice in saucepan. Add butter. Bring to a full rolling boil, a boil that does not stop bubbling when stirred, on high heat, stirring constantly. Stir in sugar. Return to a full rolling boil and boil exactly 1 minute, stirring constantly. Remove from heat. Skim foam.

Ladle immediately into prepared jars, filling to within ⅛-inch of tops.

Wipe jar rims and threads. Cover with two-piece lids. Screw bands on tightly. Place jars on rack in prepared boiling water canner. Water must cover jars by 1–2 inches. Add boiling water, if necessary. Cover; bring water to a gentle boil. Process 5 minutes. Remove jars; cool completely. When cool, check seals by pressing the middle of each lid with your finger. If a lid springs back, it is not sealed and refrigeration is necessary.

Makes 6 cups.

LEMON RASPBERRY MARMALADE

Nice spread for that toast or muffin!

4 medium-sized lemons
1¼ cups cold water
⅛ teaspoon baking soda
1 cinnamon stick
3 cups crushed fresh or frozen raspberries
7 cups granulated sugar
1 3-ounce pouch liquid fruit pectin

Wash jars in hot soapy water; rinse with hot water; drain. Wash lids following manufacturer's directions.

Zest lemons into a medium saucepan. Trim white pith from lemons; discard. Cut lemons in half and remove seeds. Chop pulp; set aside.

Add water, baking soda and cinnamon to saucepan. Bring to a boil, then reduce heat. Cover and simmer 20 minutes.

Add lemon pulp; return mixture to a boil. Reduce heat and simmer uncovered 10 minutes. Discard cinnamon stick.

Place lemon mixture into a large kettle. Add raspberries and sugar. Bring mixture to a full rolling boil, stirring constantly, and boil 2 minutes.

Quickly stir in pectin. Return to a full rolling boil. Boil 1 minute, stirring constantly. Remove from heat. Skim foam.

Immediately ladle into prepared jars, leaving ¼-inch headspace.

Add lids according to manufacturer's directions. Process in boiling water bath 10 minutes. Cool completely. When cool, check seals by pressing the middle of each lid with your finger. If a lid springs back, it is not sealed and refrigeration is necessary.

Makes 4 cups.

Sauces
Condiments

CHOCOLATE CARAMEL RASPBERRY SAUCE

Spoon sauce over pound cake or ice cream for a delicious treat.

1 14-ounce can sweetened condensed milk
25 caramels, unwrapped
4 1-ounce squares semi-sweet chocolate

2 tablespoons butter
¼ cup seedless raspberry jam

Stir sweetened condensed milk, caramels and chocolate in a heavy saucepan over low heat until smooth.

Stir in butter and raspberry jam until smooth. Serve warm. Refrigerate leftovers.

Makes 2 cups.

COOKED RASPBERRY SAUCE

Perfect sauce for that plain cheesecake!

2 10-ounce packages frozen sweetened raspberries, thawed

1 tablespoon cornstarch
¼ cup cold water

2 tablespoons granulated sugar

Heat raspberries in a heavy saucepan. Bring to a boil. Strain to remove seeds. Discard seeds.

Mix cornstarch and water in a cup until smooth. Stir into raspberry juice. Cook over medium heat until mixture comes to a boil, stirring constantly. Boil and stir 1 minute.

Remove mixture from heat. Stir in sugar. Spoon sauce into a clean glass container. Press plastic wrap onto surface of sauce; cool and refrigerate. Serve. Refrigerate leftovers.

Makes 1½ cups.

FRESH RASPBERRY SAUCE

Try this no-cook sauce over angel food cake or ice cream.

4 cups fresh raspberries, rinsed, divided
¼ cup granulated sugar
1 tablespoon raspberry flavored liqueur, optional
½ teaspoon fresh lemon juice

Process 2 cups raspberries and sugar in a food processor until pureed. Press through a fine sieve over a bowl; discard solids.

Stir in remaining 2 cups raspberries, liqueur and lemon juice. Cover and chill. Store in the refrigerator.

Makes 2 cups.

ORANGE RASPBERRY SAUCE

Top vanilla pudding, pound cake, ice cream, or your favorite dessert
with this sauce.

**1 10-ounce package frozen red raspberries in syrup, thawed,
pureed and strained; discard seeds**
⅓ cup light corn syrup
½ teaspoon fresh orange zest
¼ cup fresh orange juice

Mix all ingredients in a small bowl until well blended. Cover and refrigerate until
ready to serve. Refrigerate leftovers.

Makes 1¼ cups.

RASPBERRY CHIPOTLE SAUCE

For more heat, add a little of the adobo the chilis are packed in!

2 cups fresh or frozen unsweetened raspberries, thawed
¼ cup granulated sugar
¼ cup ruby port wine
1 chipotle chili in adobo from a 7-ounce can, or to taste

Mix all ingredients in a heavy saucepan; simmer, stirring occasionally, until sugar is dissolved; cool slightly.

Process mixture in a food processor or blender until smooth. Strain through a fine-mesh strainer to remove seeds; discard seeds. Store in the refrigerator.

Makes 1 cup.

RASPBERRY COULIS

A good sauce to use to top many desserts. Sauce can be made ahead of time and refrigerated up to 2 days.

2 6-ounce containers fresh raspberries, rinsed
¼ cup cold water
3 tablespoons superfine sugar, or as needed
2 teaspoons fresh orange or lemon juice

Process all ingredients in a blender or food processor until pureed. Push puree with a wooden spoon through a fine sieve into a small bowl; discard seeds. Taste and adjust flavor with sugar or juice if needed. Cover and chill at least one hour before serving. Refrigerate leftovers.

Makes 1 cup.

RHUBARB RASPBERRY SAUCE

A good sauce to top shortcake or ice cream.

½ cup granulated sugar
½ cup cold water

2 cups fresh rhubarb, trimmed and cut into ¼-inch pieces
1 cup fresh raspberries, rinsed and quartered

Mix sugar and water in a medium saucepan; simmer over medium-low heat until sugar is dissolved.

Add rhubarb; simmer, stirring constantly, 5 minutes. Spoon mixture into a bowl to cool. Stir in raspberries. Serve sauce at room temperature. Refrigerate leftovers.

Makes 1½ cups.

FRESH FRUIT SALSA

Fresh strawberries and raspberries are delicious in this salsa.

1 cup fresh raspberries, rinsed
1 cup diced red bell pepper
¾ cup diced green bell pepper
¾ cup hulled sliced fresh strawberries
½ cup fresh mashed strawberries
⅓ cup chopped green onion
2 tablespoons snipped fresh cilantro
2 tablespoons fresh lime juice
1 tablespoon granulated sugar
½ teaspoon salt
¼ teaspoon cracked black pepper

Mix all ingredients in a glass bowl. Cover and refrigerate several hours before serving. Store in the refrigerator.

Makes 4 cups.

RASPBERRY ONION CHUTNEY

For longer storage, follow USDA canning guidelines.

4 cups chopped yellow onion
2 cups chopped red onion
1 cup dark raisins
¼ cup fresh jalapenos, seeded and finely chopped
1½ cups brown sugar, packed
½ cup granulated sugar
1 cup balsamic vinegar
1 cup cider vinegar
2 teaspoons salt
2 tablespoons orange zest, finely grated

2 12-ounce packages frozen red raspberries, thawed

Mix all ingredients, except raspberries, in a large pot. Cover and bring mixture to a boil. Reduce heat. Remove cover and boil gently 25 minutes or until thickened, stirring occasionally.

Stir in thawed raspberries. Return mixture to a boil; boil gently 4 minutes, or until slightly thickened, without stirring.

Immediately pour hot chutney into sterilized jars. Cover and store in the refrigerator up to 2 weeks.

Makes 3 pints.

RASPBERRY SYRUP

Serve this delicious syrup on waffles and other good things.

2 cups raspberries, rinsed
1½ cups granulated sugar plus 2 tablespoons, divided

2½ cups cold water, divided
½ teaspoon fresh lemon juice

Mix raspberries, 2 tablespoons sugar and 1 cup water in a heavy medium-sized saucepan. Cook over medium heat, stirring constantly, until raspberries begin to break down and release juices, about 4 minutes.

Add 1½ cups cold water and lemon juice. Bring to a boil, then immediately reduce heat to a simmer; skim off any foam that bubbles to top. Cook 15 minutes.

Strain into a bowl through cheesecloth-lined strainer, pressing on raspberries to squeeze out juices.

Return juice to saucepan. Add 1½ cups sugar. Stir until sugar dissolves. Bring to a boil and cook 2 minutes. Remove from heat; let cool. Store syrup in a tightly sealed container in the refrigerator for up to 3 weeks.

Makes 2½ cups.

RASPBERRY SALAD DRESSING

Serve over salad greens or fruit salad.

½ **cup fresh raspberries, rinsed**
⅓ **cup raspberry vinegar**

¼ **cup granulated sugar**
2 **tablespoons Dijon-style mustard**
1 **tablespoon dairy sour cream**
1 **tablespoon minced shallots**
1 **small clove garlic, minced**
⅛ **teaspoon salt**
⅛ **teaspoon white pepper**

1¼ **cups vegetable oil**

Gently crush ½ cup raspberries in a bowl. Stir in vinegar; let stand 10 minutes. Strain raspberries; return juice to bowl. Discard seeds.

Place raspberry mixture and remaining ingredients, except vegetable oil, in a food processor fitted with a steel blade. With machine running, slowly pour in vegetable oil in a steady stream. Pour dressing into a clean glass container. Cover and store in the refrigerator.

Makes 2 cups.

RASPBERRY VINAIGRETTE

Unsweetened frozen raspberries may be used instead of fresh.

½ cup raspberry vinegar
¼ cup fresh raspberries, rinsed
¼ cup honey
½ cup fresh basil leaves

¾ cup extra virgin olive oil

Process vinegar, raspberries, honey and basil in a blender or food processor 1 minute or until blended.

With motor on, add olive oil in a slow steady stream, whirling until dressing is smooth. Pour into a clean glass container. Store in the refrigerator. Serve at room temperature.

Makes 1 cup.

RASPBERRY VINEGAR

Use vinegar within 2 weeks.

1 pint fresh raspberries, rinsed
3 cups white wine vinegar

Push raspberries through a fine-mesh sieve over a medium bowl to extract the juice; discard pulp. Pour juice into a sterilized jar. Add vinegar; shake. Cover tightly and store in the refrigerator.

Makes 3 cups.

Soup

COLD RASPBERRY SOUP

Variation: Use fresh raspberries.

4 cups frozen raspberries
¼ cup white grape juice
½ cup granulated sugar

1 cup dairy sour cream

Puree raspberries, grape juice and sugar; strain through a fine-mesh sieve and discard seeds. Pour mixture into a large bowl.

Whisk in sour cream until blended. Cover and refrigerate until chilled. Refrigerate leftovers.

Makes 4 servings.

WARM BERRY SOUP

Top this special soup with a scoop of mint gelato or ice cream.

2 tablespoons unsalted butter
4 tablespoons granulated sugar

4 cups fresh berries (1 cup each): raspberries, strawberries,
  blackberries and blueberries
juice of 2 fresh lemons
3 cups cold water
1 cup raspberry sauce

Melt butter in a large saucepan over medium heat. Whisk in sugar until blended.

Add all berries; sauté 2 minutes. Add lemon juice, water and raspberry sauce. Bring to a simmer over low heat. Remove from heat. Ladle soup into warmed bowls and serve. Serve immediately. Refrigerate leftovers.

Makes 8 servings.

About the Author

Theresa Millang is a popular and versatile cookbook author. She has written successful cookbooks on muffins, brownies, pies, cookies, cheesecake, casseroles, and several on Cajun cooking. She has cooked on television and contributed many recipes to food articles throughout the U.S.A.

Theresa's Other Cookbooks
I Love Cheesecake
I Love Pies You Don't Bake
The Muffins Are Coming
The Cookies Are Coming
The Brownies Are coming
Roux Roux Roux

Theresa's Other Current Cookbooks
The Best of Cajun-Creole Recipes
The Best of Chili Recipes
The Great Minnesota Hot Dish
The Joy of Apples
The Joy of Blueberries
The Joy of Cherries
The Joy of Cranberries
The Joy of Rhubarb
The Joy of Strawberries
The Joy of Peaches